CLOISTER

BOOKS

Cloister Books are inspired by the monastic custom of walking slowly and reading or meditating in the monastery cloister, a place of silence, centering, and calm. Within these pages you will find a similar space in which to pray and reflect on the presence of God.

Sensing God

Sensing God

Reading Scripture
With All Our Senses

Roger Ferlo

COWLEY PUBLICATIONS
Cambridge, Massachusetts

Library of Congress Cataloging-in-Publication Data:
Ferlo, Roger, 1951–
   Sensing God : reading scripture with all our senses / Roger Ferlo.
   p. cm.
   Includes bibliographical references.
   ISBN 1-56101-202-5
   1. Bible—Reading 2. Senses and sensation—Religious aspects—Christianity. I. Title.
BS617 .F47 2002
220.6—dc21   2001054351

Scripture quotations are taken from *The New Revised Standard Version* of the Bible, © 1989, by the Division of Christian Education of the National Council of the Churches of Christ in the United States of America. Used by permission.

Cynthia Shattuck, editor; Annie Kammerer, copyeditor
Vicki Black, designer
Cover art: *Disks of Newton*, 1912, by Frank Kupka
This book was printed in the United States of America by Versa Press on recycled, acid-free paper.

Cowley Publications
907 Massachusetts Avenue
Cambridge, Massachusetts 02139
800-225-1534 • www.cowley.org

For Simon Carr

You called and cried aloud and shattered my deafness. You were radiant and resplendent, you put to flight my blindness. You were fragrant, and I drew in my breath and now pant after you. I tasted you, and I feel but hunger and thirst for you. You touched me, and I am set on fire to attain the peace which is yours.

—AUGUSTINE OF HIPPO

CONFESSIONS

≈

Contents

ॐ

Acknowledgments

WRITERS OF BOOKS, even small books like this one, rely on the patience of their friends and family—listeners, informants, critics, and hand-holders. Any merits in this book I owe to them; its shortcomings, alas, are all my own. For the latter, I ask your patience. For the former, I thank David Adams, Simon Carr, Cristina Carr, Anne Richards, Lucia Kellar, Ann Monroe, George Brandt, Dr. Robert Green, Dr. Steven Tamarin, Ron Singer, Colleen McMahon, Melody Lawrence, John Merz, Sam Candler, Janet Malcolm, Maggie Robbins, Pam Foster, Peter Hawkins, Susan Wheeler, Cynthia Brome, Donald Berry, Warren Ramshaw, my wife Anne Harlan, my daughter Liz Harlan-Ferlo (who gave permission to print the poem in the final chapter of this book), my brother Patrick Ferlo (whose puzzlement about the worth of painting forced me to explain myself), my patient editor Cynthia Shattuck, her colleagues Annie Kammerer and Vicki Black, my cello teacher Allan Sher, and Dean Alan Jones, to whom this book is offered as compensation for a yet unwritten term paper on theological aesthetics, now eighteen years late.

NEW YORK CITY
MAY, 2001

XIV

❧

introduction

Sensing Scripture

ON THE COVER OF an old Lonely Planet travel guide to India there is a photograph of a man reading a book, probably a sacred text. Actually, the photograph is not of the man himself, but a close-up of one of his hands, gently resting on the book, holding it open and flat. The hand is weathered, dark, callused—yet surprisingly delicate. The fingers seem to caress the brittle, high-acid paper that, as with many books published in India, has turned a brownish-orange in the sun. Yet the Sanskrit calligraphy looks fresh, as if a pen had just left off scratching the paper. A rose blossom rests on the fold between the pages, and a small pile of blooms is gathered nearby.

The scene was no doubt carefully composed, but the blossoms are not mere decoration. Piled in heaps, worn as garlands, sold from carts, fragrant blossoms are omnipresent on the noisy Indian streets, masking the fetid stench of sewage and sweat. Perhaps the roses in the photograph were meant to cover the odor of mildew that clings to a book like this. That potent mix of glue and paper and mold and flowers would have had an impact so strong that you could have almost tasted it. You get the impression from this photograph that the act of reading the holy text engages every sense: sight, sound, touch, taste, smell.

Could we say the same if this were a Bible he was reading?

Think of all the senses you use when you pick up a Bible. What do you smell? What do you touch? What do you taste? These are odd questions, I know. For most of us reading is an activity of the eye, especially in this day of Palm Pilots and virtual books. But as much as I love my computer, I have never been able to get excited about the prospect of downloading the Bible to my laptop. Reading the Bible, after all, is not just a matter of retrieving information, or watching pixels dance across a computer screen. The experience is more than visual. The same can be said of opening any well-made book, of course. The feel of fine rag paper, the smell of glue and sizing and fresh leather, the sheer heft of the object in the hand—pleasurable sensory experiences like these are inextricably linked to the experience of reading, and are not to be dismissed lightly.

But there is more to reading scripture even than that. Reading the Bible can be an act of worship. In the ancient technique of *lectio divina,* the slow, contemplative reading of a passage of scripture—sometimes even aloud—can work like a mantra, engaging the attention of every sense. Reading scripture attentively is a matter not just of sight, but also of sound and touch, even of taste and smell.

Most of us do not associate God or the Bible with smells, at least if we are trying to think theologically. I suspect that is because most of us have been trained to think about God—and almost everything else—mainly in visual terms.

Western tradition at least as far back as Plato has always assumed that there is a hierarchy of the senses. Sight—the purest sense—is always at the top, taste and smell at the bottom. The ancients argued that of all the senses, sight allowed the greatest distance from the object perceived. It was the analytical sense *par excellence*. Baser senses like smell (and taste and touch) implied too close a contact with the material world—the world of appearances—and therefore clouded the clear perception of the Good, the True, and the Beautiful. Where sight could give control, taste and smell could overwhelm.

This favoring of the eye as the primary organ of insight has had remarkable persistence in Western thinking. Thomas Aquinas declared in his *Summa Theologica* that "saying souls understand is like saying eyes see."[1] Not noses smell, or tongues taste—understanding, says Thomas, is primarily a visual matter. The soul's organ, in effect, is the analytic eye. Such notions die hard. Four hundred years after Aquinas, at the beginning of the scientific revolution in the West, the philosopher John Locke imagined the mind as a kind of pinhole camera, a little box "wholly shut from light, with only some little opening left, to let in external visible resemblances." If the pictures so created could stay there, Locke believed (photographic film, of course, had not yet been invented), "and lie so orderly as to be found upon [demand], it would very much resemble the understanding of a man."

5

Encountering Locke's self-confident empiricism, we realize it is no accident that a common phrase in English for "I understand" is "I see." Ralph Waldo Emerson wrote in 1836:

> I become a transparent eyeball; I am nothing; I see all: the currents of the Universal Being circulate through me; I am part and parcel of God.

Emerson's ocular ego, at once charming and macabre, celebrates the Western triumph of the eye as the primary mode of perception. His remark exemplifies the egocentric yet oddly disembodied spiritual thinking that has long been the hallmark of Western religious life.

But philosophers and theologians are not necessarily our best guides in these matters. As any working painter can tell you, the experience of the visual is not just a function of the eye. Stand before a Rembrandt self-portrait or a Monet landscape and attune your eye to the artist's brush strokes. Oil paintings have a texture, a "feel," even though to protect the painting we are forbidden to touch the canvas. Trace the brush strokes with your eye or, better yet, trace them in the air with your hand, and you begin to experience in your own body the kinesthetic sensation of the painter who made the brush strokes in the first place, often centuries before. If you talk to a painter about what it is like to paint, you will most likely hear her describe what she does in rich cross-sensory terms: the pressure of the brush, the smell of the pigments and the oils, even (dangerous thing if there is lead involved) the taste of the paints. The finished painting, seemingly flat and lifeless on the wall, in fact pulsates with the traces of its creation.

This is not a book about looking at paintings. It is about sensing God through the reading of scripture. But the two experiences are more similar than you might suppose. Not just because the experience of reading a book can be tactile or olfactory, but because the very subject matter of

scripture—human contact with the Divine—
makes irresistible demands upon each of our senses if we are to understand anything at all about
God.

From the biblical viewpoint, sight is not necessarily at the top of the sensory ladder. When they
describe their experiences of God, the biblical
writers perceive a different kind of sensory hierarchy. A powerfully influential Old Testament
tradition, for example, consistently shies away
from the possibility of seeing God face to face.
God cannot be "seen" in any ordinary sense.
Only Moses had that privilege, and even for him
it was fraught with danger. On Sinai, we are told,
the Lord spoke to Moses face to face, "as one
speaks to a friend" (Exodus 33:11). But when
Moses asks God to "show me your glory," he is
only granted a glimpse of God's backside (33:18-
23). We later hear about Elijah the prophet
encountering God on that same mountain, in the
midst of fire and wind and tempest. God was not
to be seen in any of them, but rather heard—in "a
sound of sheer silence" (1 Kings 19:12).

This avoidance of face-to-face encounter with
God in the Old Testament—knowing God

through the direct evidence of the eyes—does not close off other sensory avenues to the divine. On the contrary, it often only heightens them. Perception of the divine in the Old Testament can be a multi-sensory experience—tactile, gustatory, even erotic, suffused with the memory of what Plato called "the frailer loveliness of flesh and blood." In the book of Sirach, Wisdom says of herself:

> Like cassia and camel's thorn I gave
>   forth perfume,
> and like choice myrrh I spread
>   my fragrance,
> like galbanum, onycha, and stacte,
>   and like the odor of incense in
>   the tent. . . .
> Come to me, you who desire me,
>   and eat your fill of my fruits.
>   (Sirach 24:15, 19)

Of all such texts in the Bible, it is perhaps the Song of Songs that makes the strongest appeal to all the "baser" senses:

> As an apple tree among the trees
>   of the wood,

so is my beloved among young men.
With great delight I sat in his shadow,
  and his fruit was sweet to my taste.
He brought me to the banqueting house,
  and his intention toward me was love.
Sustain me with raisins,
  refresh me with apples;
  for I am faint with love.
O that his left hand were under my head,
  and that his right hand embraced me!
I adjure you, O daughters of Jerusalem,
  by the gazelles or the wild does:
do not stir up or awaken love until it
  is ready!   (Song of Solomon 2:3-7)

9

This is not a poem about seeing, but about tasting, smelling, touching. Can it really be about God? Its sensual specificity has challenged pious readers from the beginning. A text like the Song of Solomon would be often ruthlessly allegorized: God is the lover, the bride is the church; it is a poem not about earthly love but heavenly redemption. And just as the text was allegorized in order to contain its emotional pull, so were the senses themselves—the senses to which this passage appeals so powerfully. There was a deep conviction on the part of early Christian thinkers that the five senses, in the words of a present-day theologian, "are but the fall and scattering of an original and richly abundant capacity to observe God and divine things."[2] Not even sight was exempt from such a fall. Thus reading the text allegorically could be understood as an attempt to restore this original transparency of sensory perception—to return us to a paradise where God could be observed as God is, not as our fallen senses would like God to be.

But even the most relentless allegorizing cannot distance the reader completely from the sensuous attraction of these Old Testament images for God. The powerful tension between distance and desire forces readers of these Old Testament texts to engage the full range of human emotion in describing their own experiences of God— experiences that call on every one of the senses even as their inadequacies are exposed. And if the testimony of Moses and Elijah and the writers of Wisdom and the Song of Solomon can be believed, sight—of all the senses—is the one least likely to get us very far.

10

The New Testament writers share the Old Testament's ambivalence toward the evidence of the eyes. But the New Testament writers also emphasize the experience of God through the other senses. The prologue to John's gospel quotes Exodus 33 with ringing certainty: "No one has ever seen God" (1:18). The Jesus John presents to his readers interacts with his disciples and intimates in memorably sensual ways. His friend Mary of Bethany theatrically anoints him for burial, wiping his feet with her hair. The disciple "whom Jesus loved" rests his head against Jesus' chest as they are gathered for their final supper. Where the synoptic gospels have Jesus feeding his friends with bread and wine that he declares to be his body and blood, John has Jesus instead perform that most tactile of actions—washing the sandy feet of his disciples. After his resurrection Jesus invites Thomas to thrust his hand into his side, and shares in a fish-fry on the beach. All this in a gospel that is the most self-conscious of the four in presenting Jesus in full, untouchable divinity.

Even in Paul's writings, influenced as they seem to be by Platonic thought, sight is not the most reliable path to the full experience of God:

> For now we see in a mirror, dimly, but then we will see face to face. Now I know only in part; then I will know fully, even as I have been fully known. (1 Corinthians 13:12)

As in Plato, here seeing and knowing are all but synonymous. Yet where Plato's exemplary seeker can achieve access to divine knowledge through an arduous education of sight, Paul's best efforts at seeing God achieve knowledge that is only partial—"in a mirror, dimly." The Christian seeker of the divine comes to full insight not by a gradual emergence from Plato's dark cave of ignorance toward the light of knowledge, but by a sudden apocalyptic revelation at the end of time, when all things will become clear in Christ.

As both Paul and the gospel writers proclaimed, it is not just on the evidence of the eyes that God is revealed in the world. Jesus of Nazareth lived and walked and breathed and ate and touched and heard and spoke. God enfleshed was God possessed of every human sense—and like every human being, Jesus was capable of being touched and heard and seen and smelled. Speaking as an eyewitness to Jesus (which Paul was not), the writer of John's letters could claim not only that his eyes had seen the Word made flesh, but that his hands had handled it (1 John 1:1).

These early congregations of believers lived in a deeply sensuous world, one in which the presence of God was experienced by means of all the senses working together—the taste of bread and wine, the smell of incense, the touch of the laying on of hands in prayer. Even reading the word of God in scripture was less a visual than an aural experience. Scripture was written to be read aloud, and is grasped best when heard rather than seen. The word of God in scripture would have been incomprehensible outside the full experience of what we might today call a sacramental life. Reading scripture was never an end in itself, never divorced from the multiple bodily sensations that were the hallmarks of Christian practice.

Try to imagine yourself being initiated into one of those ancient assemblies. Hearing scripture is only the beginning. You can enter into the full knowledge of Christ only by undertaking a set of actions that challenge every sense, beginning with a harrowing immersion in the waters of baptism. In that cold pool, every nerve ending awakened by the flow and pressure of living water, you experience the touch of Christ "in you," as Paul himself put it. Surrounded by other Christians holding torches in the darkness, you can see very little, but you feel everything: the smooth oil of anointing pouring down your forehead; the gentle touch of hands drying and clothing your body; the coolness of the linen draped around you as you "put on Christ." You smell the pungent aroma of olives and balsam. And finally, you taste the bread broken and the cup shared, taking Christ's flesh and blood into your own body, becoming a living temple of the Lord.

In our own day, the closest many Christians come to this kind of cross-sensory religious experience may be in celebrating the Great Vigil of Easter. At the start of that ancient liturgy, scripture becomes once again an intensely aural experience—lesson after lesson is read aloud in the darkness, the newly lit paschal candle the only source of light. Then, still in darkness, solemn promises are made, and bodies jostle one another as they make their way to the font. There is the sound of water poured, the smell of incense burning. By its own dim light you can watch as the huge beeswax candle, pierced with five grains of incense, is dipped three times into the font. The smell of incense mingles with the scent of chrism as the newly baptized feel the oil of anointing on their foreheads. A single voice intones the Great Alleluia, and the church, suddenly filled with light, echoes with bells and organ and song. At a service like this, scripture is less read than enacted: not just seen and heard, but felt and smelled and even, in the sharing of eucharistic bread and wine, tasted as well. "Your words were found," says the prophet Jeremiah, "and I ate them" (15:16).

What I am describing here runs counter to our modern sensibility concerning the appropriate use of scripture. Since the Reformation, particularly in the West, Christians of all traditions have often tended to think about scripture as a kind of information manual. We tend to read scripture for the facts (to find out what actually happened) and for the rules (to find out what exactly we are supposed to do about what happened). But to read scripture for information only is to risk missing the sense of it all—sense not only as cognitive meaning but also as meaning felt and touched. My eyes have seen the Word made flesh, says the writer of John's first epistle, and my hands have handled it. It is said that doctors in ancient times used to recommend reading as a physical exercise to their patients, on a par with walking, running, or ball-playing.[3] In this spirit, I wonder whether we might begin to adopt a more sensorily integrated way of reading scripture, particularly the New Testament—a way of reading, grounded in the sacramental life, that restores, so to speak, the body to the text.

In each of the chapters that follow, I try to approach an episode in the New Testament writings by means of a particular sense, beginning in the first chapter with smell, and ending with hearing and sight. The order is intentional. Ending with sound and sight is not meant to reassert their traditional priority. On the contrary, it is an attempt to mediate the experience of hearing and seeing Jesus—whether as a contemporary eyewit-

ness, or as a present-day reader of scripture—
through the more intimate senses of smell and
touch and taste. This approach might come as no
surprise to readers who are lovers of painting or
music. Try your hand at playing the cello or
working in oils and you quickly sense how tightly the experience of sound and sight is linked to
the touch of flesh on fingerboard or brush on canvas. To listen to a cello suite or to gaze at a painting without some regard for this cross-sensory
interplay is to suffer a terrible impoverishment.

17

The same is true in our attempts to encounter
the divine in reading scripture. Centuries ago,
Ignatius of Loyola urged readers of scripture to
participate in the life of Christ through a disci-
plined use of all the senses. When reading a story
from the gospels, like the healing of Peter's mother-in-law, Ignatius tells us to enter the scene fully
and to become each character in turn:

> With the eyes of the imagination we should
> look ... at the persons. With our hearing
> we should perceive how they are speaking
> or could speak. With the sense of smell and
> taste we should smell and taste the infinite
> sweetness and loveliness of the Godhead.

With our sense of place we should embrace
and kiss the place where these persons have
set their foot and where they come to rest.[4]

It is in that Ignatian spirit, alive to the evidence—
and the pleasures—of the senses, that these meditations are written.

18

*We declare to you what was from the
beginning, what we have heard, what we
have seen with our eyes, what we have
looked at and touched with our hands,
concerning the word of life—this life was
revealed, and we have seen it and testify to
it, and declare to you the eternal life that
was with the Father and was revealed to
us—we declare to you what we have seen
and heard so that you also may have fellowship with us; and truly our fellowship is
with the Father and with his Son Jesus
Christ.*　　　　　　　(1 JOHN 1:1-3)

꒜

one

The Smell of God

BEGIN, IF YOU CAN, by smelling a story.

While he was at Bethany in the house of Simon the leper, as he sat at the table, a woman came with an alabaster jar of very costly ointment of nard, and she broke open the jar and poured the ointment on his head. But some were there who said to one another in anger, "Why was the ointment wasted in this way? For this ointment could have been sold for more than three hundred denarii, and the money given to the poor." And they scolded her. But Jesus said, "Let her alone; why do you trouble her? She has performed a good service for me. For you always have the poor with you, and you can show kindness to them whenever you wish; but you will not always have me. She has done what she could; she has anointed my body beforehand for its burial. Truly I tell you, wherever the good news is proclaimed in the whole world, what she has done will be told in remembrance of her." (Mark 14:3-9)

Who is this woman, anyway? She has no name, no history. Where does she come from? What prompts her to do what she does? What makes the bystanders object to her presence so strongly? In Luke's version of the story, their objections are understandable—a prostitute has broken into the house of righteous people, interrupting a proper banquet in an attempt to justify herself. But in Mark, the objection is not to the woman (it is hard to be improper in a leper's house), but to the waste of expensive ointment. And the sign of that waste was the overwhelming smell.

Why was the ointment wasted in this way, they ask, when the money could have been given to the poor? They know the spikenard is expensive, but this is not the only thing that makes them angry. Why should Jesus, friend of the poor, insist that the woman's extravagant act of homage has done him "good service"? What does he mean by the peculiarly oracular pronouncement that "what she has done will be told in remembrance of her"? In memory of *her*? She doesn't even have a name. She doesn't even speak. She has ruined their supper. She has filled the room with an ungodly stench. And Jesus has praised her for it. What is going on here? What kind of world is this?

To answer such questions, that is, to enter this story as the story demands, you have to attend to the smell of it. To put it bluntly, you have to wake up and smell the spikenard. You have to think not in words but in smell, and smell has a logic all its own.

You can read a lot about nard—commonly called spikenard—in books. You can learn its formal Latin title, *Nardostachys jatamansi,* and its chemical constituents—bornyl acetate, isobornyl valerianate, borneol, patchouli alcohol, terpinyl valerianate, eugenol, pinene. The aromatherapy handbook I have here on my desk assures me that spikenard will quell my fear and anxiety, improve my meditations, and induce restful sleep and pleasant dreams. The ancient Egyptians prized it as a means of appeasing the gods. The Bible associates it with both kingship and erotic love, a heady mixture. The poet of the Song of Solomon sings:

> While the king was on his couch,
>   my nard gave forth its fragrance.
> My beloved is to me a bag of myrrh
>   that lies between my breasts.
>   (Song of Solomon 1:12-13)

Did Mark have passages like this in mind as he meditated on the incident? (And is that why Luke associated the story with a prostitute?) In the Old Testament, kings are anointed, not crowned, just as Jesus is anointed in Mark's story. But paradoxically, both scripture and local custom also associated such fragrant oils as myrrh and spikenard with the embalming of the dead—an ominous topic amid talk of kingship. "She has done what she could; she has anointed my body beforehand for its burial."

It is one thing to know all this about spikenard. It is quite another actually to smell it. A friend of mine once loaned me a tiny vial of the stuff, purchased at a local health shop. Once I managed to crack the seal, the first whiff made me gasp for air. To me, at least, the smell is anything but soothing. It is, in the words of my aromatherapy manual, piercing, earthy, animal-like, "reminiscent of goats." No wonder people in Simon's house were angry. When that mysterious woman suddenly broke the seal on her alabaster jar, and that goat-like stench permeated every inch of the room, conversation would have stopped, eating would have become impossible. There was no escaping her or her smells. Every thought, every emotion, every action would have had to center on the implacable odor and all that it represented—healing, intimacy, kingship, burial.

Entering the banquet room uninvited and unannounced, this woman violated a boundary, and not just the boundary separating invited guest from unwelcome stranger. In pouring this ointment over Jesus' head—an ointment whose piercing smell was associated not only with sleep and dreams but also with the fate of kings—the woman ushered the assembled guests across the threshold into a dangerous no-man's-land. By the time the story ends, at Calvary and the rock-hewn tomb, everyone in the room, including Jesus, would come to know that land by the smell of it.

Smells are all about thresholds. Say you come across a perfumed advertisement as you read a glossy magazine. For some people, and not just those with allergies, an ad like that can stop reading in its tracks, the distraction is so overwhelming and annoying. But the advertisers are betting that such people would be in the minority. What they hope is that for most people the smell will linger pleasantly just below the threshold of consciousness as they continue to read, predisposing them to buy the scent and wear it. The appeal is subliminal (literally, "below the threshold," from the Latin word *limen*). If the ad agency has done its market research wisely, the effect will last.

But smell can be a sign not just of the subliminal, which tends to be subtle and covert, but also of the boldly liminal. In every culture, certain kinds of smell—the smell of spikenard is a good example—function in a charged moment like the one at Simon's house as powerful warning signs. We know that we have come to a critical threshold, and important things are at stake. Cultural anthropologists tell us that such smells are especially important as markers in rites of passage—between puberty and adulthood, between life and death.[1] In a puberty rite, a neophyte might be forced to smell "dirty"—to become neither fish nor fowl—as an outward sign of his yet-to-be-defined place in the adult world he is about to enter.

Smells are most noticeable at boundaries—boundaries both physical and emotional. We pause, however briefly, before entering a room or space if it smells different from the place where we are standing. To smell an odor from an unknown source (or from a source you fear) is to allow it to become part of us—or threaten to become part of us—in ways that we cannot predict. Smells can be at once attractive and threatening, because smells contain within themselves physical traces of the object being smelled. We either flee the smell or enter it. Or rather, for such is the nature of smells, it enters us. The reaction is immediate, and not always in our control. We cannot linger for long at thresholds.

I had the good fortune to grow up in a religious tradition where smells were omnipresent during worship: the smell of incense and melting beeswax, the smell of wine in a cruet or of balsam mixed with olive oil for anointing and chrismation. But the smells of a Catholic boyhood were as nothing compared to what I once encountered when I visited the state of Tamil Nadu in South India. The smell of coconut and mangoes spread out in *puja* offerings. The smell of melted butter slathered on a shiny Shiva *lingam*. The pervasive smell of marigold and jasmine blossoms, worn as garlands around the necks of worshipers, or draped on statues of the gods, or heaped high in great conical piles in the marketplace. Worship in India was as much about smell (and touch and taste) as it was about sight or sound.

I had an unexpected kind of threshold experience at the very start of my stay in India, one that in fact had nothing directly to do with religion. My family had arrived as few people do these

days, by student ship. My wife and I were travel-
ing around the world as teachers. More by chance
than design, the itinerary followed the track of
European conquest in the southern hemisphere—
from Salvador in Brazil across the South Atlantic
to the Cape of Good Hope, north to Kenya, and
finally northeast to India and South Asia. In our
brief, four-day stop in Madras (since renamed
Chenai), I had made elaborate plans to take a bus
trip to visit the great shore temples of seventh-
century Mahabalapuram, and then to get a taste
of village life by spending a few days in Erode, a
small town about two hundred miles to the west.
To get to Mahabalapuram, you have to travel
along the Beach Road that hugs the Bay of
Bengal, at the place where the sprawling city the
British built reaches the margins of the ancient
sea. I had read my guidebook, and knew that the
route would take us past the old Mar Thoma
Cathedral, where the remains of St. Thomas the
Apostle are said to repose, and then past the little
Anglican church that nestles beside it. I knew, too,
that as we proceeded south of the city toward the
suburbs we would pass by the even more ancient
St. Thomas's Mount. People say that Thomas was

killed kneeling on a stone that now serves as the central altar of the old church standing there.

To approach these ancient holy places, Christian and Hindu, by the Beach Road from the port meant that I first had to cross the Cooum River on the Napier Bridge. Like most first-time visitors from the West, I had both romanticized and exoticized this passage into India. I was on a kind of intellectual pilgrimage, well-read on the subject, attuned to the importance of crossings and thresholds—crossing cultures, crossing languages, crossing religions. But a first visit to India (or even a tenth) is notorious for overturning intellectual expectations. I was with friends on a noisy tour bus. Suddenly there came a moment, as we made our way along the coast toward the bridge, when everyone stopped talking, confused, breathing heavily. Nothing was said, because nothing needed to be said. The river was an open sewer. The stench of human waste seemed to penetrate the flesh. My fellow travelers and I looked at each other in disbelief, too polite to comment, or perhaps just too stunned, refusing to admit to ourselves that we smelled what we were smelling. In crossing through that stench I had been forced across a threshold—a threshold separating romantic fantasy from complex fact. I had come to a place where my usual categories of clean and dirty, beauty and waste, were all mixed up, where the smell of jasmine and the stench of excrement wantonly intermingled. Thinking I knew everything I needed to know about India, that river crossing warned me that in fact I knew next to nothing at all. I had been forced to begin to think in smells.

In revealing such facts about boundaries, smell exhibits its own inexorable logic. It also creates its own mythology. Take an ancient example, one that seems as far removed from the world of late twentieth-century India as India seems removed from the world of the New Testament writers. In the *Metamorphoses*, the Roman poet Ovid tells the disturbing story of Myrrha, from whom myrrh gets its name. A young and beautiful princess, she falls in love with her father, King Cinyras of Cyprus. Driven by a passion that she cannot control, she contrives a way to make love to him in disguise. With characteristic irony, Ovid has her do this during the festival of Ceres, a nine-day harvest feast during which married women like her mother abstain from sex. Discovering his daughter's treachery, the king seeks to kill her. Pregnant with her father's child, she flees his kingdom, and as she runs away she is transformed into a myrrh tree. Nine months later, from a crack in the tree, the god Adonis is born. He is reared by naiads, who anoint him with his mother's tears, now transformed into odoriferous sap, the source of royal incense used in fragrant offering to the gods. Thus a sacred fragrance—the means of bridging the distance between the human and divine—derives from the breaking of an incest taboo, the terrible violation of a fearsome boundary.

Like many such stories in Ovid, this is a highly elaborated and sophisticated version of a simple "Just So" story, like the one about how the elephant got its trunk. Why does the smell of myrrh have such religious power? Myrrh evokes at once the memory of death (the incest with Cinyras, the death of Myrrha) and the promise of life (the birth of Adonis, the nurturing sap of the myrrh tree). As Rousseau would put it centuries later, smell is the sense of imagination and desire. In Ovid's hands, desire is mixed with memory.

With sacred smells like myrrh and spikenard, the memory evoked is the memory of death, and the desire to which such memories are inextricably linked is the desire for immortality—to become an Adonis, to become like God.

The gospel writers, working within a biblical tradition associating smells with matters divine, come to similar conclusions. "Like cassia and camel's thorn I gave forth perfume," says Divine Wisdom, "and like choice myrrh I spread my fragrance" (Sirach 24:15). It is no accident that myrrh figures both in the story of Jesus' birth (where Matthew counts it among the gifts of the magi) and in the stories of his burial, where spices like myrrh are used to embalm his corpse. No wonder the unnamed woman in Mark, cracking open her alabaster jar, unleashes a sacred odor at the very moment when the gospel brings Jesus to the threshold of his passion, death, and resurrection.

Perhaps it seems blasphemous to go to Hindu India, and then to pagan Rome, to interpret so important a gospel episode as the anointing of Jesus. But to enter the gospel stories through all five senses demands unusual preparation. We must fight against the anti-sensory prejudice that pervades our religious culture, one that considers the pleasures of the senses somehow antithetical to the experience of God. Catholic and Orthodox Christian worshipers have an advantage over other Christians in this regard. In their liturgies, the solemn reading of scripture is often accompanied by the rich smell of incense. Intoned at the "crossing" of aisle and transept, or before the polychromed wall of the iconostasis at the threshold of the sacred space, the sung Word engulfs us: we see it, hear it, smell it. Such a wanton mixture of sensory experience rubs against the modern religious grain. For Protestant Christians especially, products of a reformed sensibility that prefers to receive the Word exclusively through the eye and the ear, the logic of smell can seem downright opaque.

But from the point of view of the earliest Christians, this modern narrowing of the sensorium is an aberration. The paradoxical logic of smells was a marker of early Christian experience. In the period when Paul wrote his letters and Mark wrote his gospel, the word "Christ" itself carried with it the pungent memory of a sacred smell. "Christ" is the Greek equivalent of the

Hebrew word "Messiah"—"the anointed one." Both words evoke the fragrant memory of oil against skin. To say the word "Christ" was to evoke the smell and feel of an anointing. Baptism and anointing in the name of the Messiah accomplished many things, but one of them was that it made you *smell* like a Christian. Smeared with the oil of anointing, the new Christian bridged the Great Divide between the human and the divine, and between life and death.

33

This is what Paul means in 2 Corinthians when he speaks of Christ leading Christians like a Roman conqueror in triumphal procession, spreading through them

> in every place the fragrance that comes from knowing him. For we are the aroma of Christ to God among those who are being saved and among those who are perishing; to the one a fragrance from death to death, to the other a fragrance from life to life.   (2 Corinthians 2:14-16)

"We are the aroma of Christ": a present-day anthropologist of the senses would readily understand Paul's turn of phrase. What may seem to us a mere figure of speech (how can we *be* the "aroma" of Christ?) is grounded in particular sensory experiences that carry inklings of divine presence. For the Christian, in Paul's thinking, the fragrance of Christ is a marker of a radical change of status. Like the incense in the temple that bears the prayers of the priest to God, the baptized and anointed believer now bears the fragrance of Christ to the world. That fragrance, like all smells at the threshold, possesses a double meaning, and wields a double effect. To those who have been saved, that is, to those who bear the aroma of Christ on their persons, the pleasing smell of Paul's Corinthian followers now matches their own, a signal that they are welcome in the new community of believers. But to those who are perishing, to those who have refused baptism in Christ Jesus, the aroma of Christ among Paul's followers is perceived as an offense and a scandal. They will experience it as the stench of death, as a death leading to another death.

To our modern ears, Paul's mode of argument may seem forced, even macabre. But this is not an argument for the ear. For people who are accustomed to thinking in smells, Paul's logic seems natural. It is a logic savored in the nostrils, absorbed through the skin.

One of the several paradoxes in Mark's story of the anointing (and, for that matter, in Luke's and Matthew's) is that smell is everywhere present and nowhere mentioned. It is like the purloined letter in Poe's short story, hidden in plain sight. Not so in John's version, where the all-pervasive smell of costly ointment occupies the center of the episode's sensory world:

> Six days before the Passover Jesus came to Bethany, the home of Lazarus, whom he had raised from the dead. There they gave a dinner for him. Martha served, and Lazarus was one of those at table with him. Mary took a pound of costly perfume made of pure nard, anointed Jesus' feet, and wiped them with her hair. The house was filled with the fragrance of the perfume.
>
> (John 12:1-3)

Where Mark presents a woman without a name, and Luke describes her only as a prostitute, John memorably identifies her as one of Jesus' closest friends, Mary of Bethany. In so doing, he sets the scene not in the home of an outcast leper, where the woman's transgression of boundaries might be expected, or of a Pharisee, where such transgressions would be deplored, but in the home of Lazarus, Mary's brother, whom Jesus had just raised from the dead. (If Mark and Luke, who also set the scene in Bethany, know how important a place it was in Jesus' private and public life, they do not let on.) The family members of Lazarus in Bethany are central figures in John's story, though almost completely absent from the other gospels. What's more, Mary's dramatic gesture—linked forever to the odor that fills the house—does not meet with general objection (no surprise, as this is Mary's own house, after all). In John's telling of the story, it is Judas Iscariot—and Judas only—who expresses disgust: "Why was this perfume not sold for three hundred denarii and the money given to the poor?" (12:5).

Judas sets his scheme of betrayal in motion the very next day. It is as if the stench of the ointment pushes him to decisive action. Judas's distrust of smell is the narrative equivalent of his need to quantify and control Christ's generosity, poured out as freely as Mary's ointment. The narrator's cruel aside explaining Judas's motives casts this quantifying impulse in the most negative light possible: "He said this not because he cared about the poor, but because he was a thief" (12:6). The aside echoes Paul's indictment of "peddlers" of the truth: "For we are the aroma of Christ... not peddlers of God's word like so many" (2 Corinthians 2:15, 17). Judas, of course, is the ultimate peddler. In Matthew's version of the story, Judas sells Jesus out for thirty pieces of silver, the value of an injured slave, but John chooses a different tack. As Judas seeks to contain the overwhelming stench of the ointment within its proper bounds, it drives him across the very threshold of betrayal.

Jesus seems to know this—the smell of Mary's ointment points the way to Judas's treachery. But it also points in another direction, back to a resurrection that has already occurred—Jesus' raising of Lazarus from the dead. In fact, the story of Lazarus raised and the story of his sister anointing Jesus for burial are two parts of the same story, one that points us forward toward a still-greater story: the story of Jesus' own resurrection.

And there may be one further story evoked here about the smell of death and thresholds crossed. It is the story of the Exodus, of Israel's liberation from bondage in Egypt—a liberation that prefigures the liberation of John's own readers through the power of Jesus' death and resurrection. The connection is subtle, but haunting, evoked by the resonance of a single Greek word, and again it has to do with smell. Here is how John describes Jesus' approach to the tomb of Lazarus:

> It was a cave, and a stone lay upon it. Jesus said, Take ye away the stone. Martha, the sister of him that was dead, saith unto him, Lord, by this time he stinketh: for he hath been dead four days. (John 11:38-39, KJV)

I quote the King James translation from 1611 here because the coarseness of the Jacobean diction ("he stinketh") faithfully reflects the tone of the unusual Greek word John uses. In the New Testament, this word *ozo* occurs only here. It is just as rare in the Greek version of the Old Testament known to the gospel writers. There, too, *ozo* occurs only once. It describes the stench of the frogs called down as a plague upon Pharaoh's house, piled up and rotting on the banks of the Nile: "And they gathered them together upon heaps: and the land stank" (Exodus 8:14, KJV).

There is no reason to think that the writer of John chose this word specifically because it occurs in Exodus, but the coincidence is powerful. The stink of the frogs placed Israel on the threshold of liberation from bondage in Egypt. So, too, the stink of Lazarus's rotting corpse leads the reader, almost by the nose, to his miraculous liberation from the bonds of death and the grave. In both stories, the stench of death reveals a fearsome boundary to be crossed. The miraculous crossing from death to life celebrated in Exodus is given new life and form at Lazarus's tomb. It is no accident that John places the episode of Jesus' anointing immediately following the story of Lazarus's return to life. The passion story in John is the Exodus story retold. The stink of death gives way to the fragrance of life, the rotting corpse to the anointed body—to the very smell of God.

39

ᔧ

You shall also take the fat of the ram, the
fat tail, the fat that covers the entrails, the
40   *appendage of the liver, the two kidneys*
with the fat that is on them, and the right
thigh (for it is a ram of ordination), and
one loaf of bread, one cake of bread made
with oil, and one wafer, out of the basket of
unleavened bread that is before the LORD;
and you shall place all these on the palms
of Aaron and on the palms of his sons, and
raise them as an elevation offering before
the LORD. *Then you shall take them from*
their hands, and turn them into smoke on
the altar on top of the burnt offering of
pleasing odor before the LORD; *it is an*
offering by fire to the LORD.

(EXODUS 29:22-25)

We are the aroma of Christ. . . .

(2 CORINTHIANS 2:15)

two

The Taste
of God

WE DO NOT USUALLY think of the apostle Paul as a
sensuous man. Judging by his letters, the bodily
senses were unimportant to him. Taste, smell,
touch, even sound and sight—these were earthly
sensations to be left aside as he and his followers
awaited their imminent departure for the heavenly kingdom. Perhaps unfairly, Paul has a reputa-
tion as something of a gnostic—a theologian who

lived too much in his head, and when push came to shove, would rather leave the body and all its distractions behind.

So you have to wonder, did Paul know the story we have just heard about Mary and the ointment? Did he know about Lazarus coming back from the dead? For that matter, did he know any stories about Jesus at all—Jesus the living, breathing, feeling human being? Paul quotes Jesus, but only sparingly, and he remains strangely mute about almost all the stories told about Jesus, and all the stories that Jesus told. Had he not heard them? Did the Christians who had instructed Paul after his conversion know nothing about these things? Or was he too much an intellectual to be concerned with the folksy particulars of story-telling, or too otherworldly to care?

The situation is all the more remarkable because Paul's preaching is anchored so firmly in Jesus' body—its death and resurrection. No one matches Paul when it comes to preaching the passion of Christ: "For I decided to know nothing among you except Jesus Christ, and him crucified" (1 Corinthians 2:2). Paul claimed direct knowledge of Jesus, even though he himself was not one of the original eyewitnesses. Direct knowledge without seeing? An odd claim. No wonder so many of Jesus' surviving followers distrusted Paul. Given the opposition he faced from the apostle James and his friends in Jerusalem, one would think that the meticulous accounts of the events leading to the passion that we read in the gospels would provide Paul with some of his best preaching material. But of these powerful episodes—the anointing at Bethany, the cleansing of the temple, the foot-washing, the trial, the flogging, Calvary, the garden tomb—Paul says not a word. Not a word about Judas. Very little about Peter. Not a word about Mary Magdalene or Joseph of Arimathea or the disciple whom Jesus loved. Nothing about people or places or times or motives. No drama, no particulars.

There is, however, one spectacular exception:

For I received from the Lord what I also handed on to you, that the Lord Jesus on the night when he was betrayed took a loaf of bread, and when he had given thanks, he broke it and said, "This is my body that is for you. Do this in remembrance of me." In the same way he took the cup also, after supper, saying, "This cup is the new covenant in my blood. Do this, as often as you drink it, in remembrance of me." For as often as you eat this bread and drink the cup, you proclaim the Lord's death until he comes. (1 Corinthians 11:23-26)

It is typical of Paul that he claims that his knowledge of what Jesus said and did at the Last Supper comes directly "from the Lord." Even if he could have read Luke or John on the subject, I suspect he would not have admitted it. From the time of his conversion, Paul had remained prickly about his status as an equal among the apostles. He was not among the original twelve. He was not an eyewitness to events. He never saw Jesus face to face in the flesh. As he himself put it, he was the last of the apostles, a follower untimely born, and he seemed to know that this late arrival was being held against him by his opponents. Yet from the moment of his conversion and call, he claimed immediate knowledge of the risen Jesus, knowledge as direct and firsthand as anything claimed by James or Peter or Andrew. So when he says that what he knows comes directly "from the Lord," you want to grant him his point, if only

44

because this letter to the Corinthians from which we have just read is the earliest written document we have recounting anything of consequence about Jesus' life. Mark's gospel, thought by many to be the first written, dates from the 60s and 70s at the earliest, at least ten years after this letter of Paul's appeared. No written evidence is closer to Jesus' own day. Paul's report has the earmarks of urgency and freshness.

So what do we make of it? Of the scores of episodes that people remembered from the life of Jesus, what would have attracted Paul to the story of the Last Supper? Or, if he knew no other episodes than this, what did he see in it? How would this episode move his hearers "to know Jesus Christ, and him crucified"? How could anyone claim to know Jesus without hearing the rest of the story?

Perhaps we are asking the wrong questions. Maybe Paul and his followers did not miss the stories about Jesus because they did not really need them. In the charged ritual acts of washing, anointing, singing, hearing, and eating, their liturgies fleshed out the gospel of the cross with compelling immediacy. Maybe they did not need the story because *they* were the story.

I think this is why Paul denounces the Corinthians' misconduct at the Lord's supper so violently. "For all who eat and drink without discerning the body," he warns the Corinthians, "eat and drink judgment against themselves. For this reason many of you are weak and ill, and some have died" (11:29-30). Could Paul have really believed this? Did he really think that people would sicken and die if they shared the Lord's supper unworthily? Perhaps he was only speaking rhetorically—speaking, as it were, to deadly effect. If a significant number of Corinthians were falling ill or dropping dead after participating in the eucharist, surely the cause of all this grief would be explicable in epidemiological terms. A contaminant in the wine perhaps, or worms in the bread. But eating unworthily? Treating each other shabbily? Failing to discern the body? Could this really kill you?

Whose body is he talking about, anyway? Is it Jesus' own body—blood and bones and sinews— that can be tasted in the bread and wine? This seems unlikely, even for Paul. Communion bread tastes like bread—sour, chewy, crusty—and communion wine tastes like wine—sweet, heady, tangy. Even later believers in transubstantiation concede as much. When Christians come together for the eucharist, they are sipping wine, not blood; chewing bread, not tasting roasted flesh. It is the same in our time as it was in Paul's. So perhaps he is talking not about "discerning" Christ's *physical* body, but rather Christ's *mystical* body, understood as the community of those who worship him.

> When you come together, it is not really to eat the Lord's supper. For when the time comes to eat, each of you goes ahead with your own supper, and one goes hungry and another becomes drunk. (11:20-21)

Rich people, having the leisure to arrive early and the wherewithal to eat well, exclude poor people from the table, humiliating those who have nothing. They are guilty of inflicting a kind of social death, gravely injuring the body politic.

This makes sense sociologically. Taste is a private experience. No one tastes anything in exactly the same way. But eating in company makes this most intimate of senses a public affair. A wrong move like eating someone else's portion by mistake, or eating in front of someone, or using the wrong fork, or saying the wrong thing at the wrong time and offending the person next to us or even the entire group—this can make us feel sick, turning food to ashes in our mouths.

48

But it will not kill us. We might be mortified about our misbehavior—and mortification, as its Latin root implies, is a kind of dying. But the death Paul talks about is not just mortification. The Corinthians are in danger of more than social death. The bread and wine offered in Jesus' name has an intrinsic power both to heal and to kill. To understand Paul rightly is to enter a world where maladies of the spirit manifest themselves as maladies of the flesh. In the wrong hands and shared in the wrong circumstances, bread and wine consecrated in Jesus' name can work like poison. "For this reason many of you are weak and ill, and some have died." Perhaps it is just a metaphor. But we cannot eat metaphors. Metaphors do not poison us. Can the taste of God, like the sight of God, be fatal?

Taste—at least in religious terms—is a more complex sense than we usually give it credit for. Physiologically, of course, it is linked to smell. If our sense of smell is compromised, our sense of taste suffers. Anyone who has tried to savor a visually enticing dish of pasta while suffering the effects of a cold knows what this means. But taste is also linked to smell emotionally. Like smell, taste mixes memory and desire in ways sometimes too immediate for comfort.

To talk of taste in this way is to regard it as a way of knowing. Imagine biting into a plum for the very first time. From that day forward, we have a knowledge of "plumness" that cannot be had in any other way.[1] Such knowledge is closely linked to remembrance. It is what Proust describes in the famous opening pages of his novel *In Search of Lost Time*. On a visit to his mother's house, Marcel is offered a morsel of biscuit—called *madeleine*—soaked in lime-blossom tea. At the first moment of tasting, he is engulfed by memories of childhood in the village of Combray, and his aunt Leonie, now long dead, who had often served him the same little meal:

When from a long-distant past nothing
subsists, after the people are dead, after the
things are broken and scattered, taste and
smell alone, more fragile but more endur-
ing, more unsubstantial, more persistent,
more faithful, remain poised a long time,
like souls, remembering, waiting, hoping,
amid the ruins of all the rest; and bear
unflinchingly, in the tiny and almost impal-
pable drop of their essence, the vast structure of recollection.[2]

Proust's vast structure of recollection extends
to six immense volumes of autobiographical fic-
tion. Most of us are not so prolific, nor our taste-
memories so momentous. When I was a child, I
used to spend long, hot summer afternoons with
my grandmother in the washhouse of her truck
farm—a vegetable and flower farm—in central
New York State. In her kitchen, my grandmother
was the gentlest, kindest of women, but in the
washhouse she was all business. Watching her
work was intimidating. Seated in a dark corner
for hours on end, humorless and focused, she
would pull out handful after handful of scallions
from a massive metal washtub. With a dexterity

50

that alarmed me, she would tie each new bunch with a small length of string plucked from a skein attached to her belt, then toss each shining bundle onto an ever-growing pile that my grandfather would deliver before dawn next day to the farmer's market in Utica. My grandmother has been dead for three decades. The truck farm has long since been sold off, its fields abandoned, the washhouse left derelict. But a crisp bite of scallion returns me to that long-lost time and place with uncanny speed. My grandmother, stern in her cool, shaded corner, an old kerchief tied around her head. The immense washtub with its tangle of hoses. The homemade skein of string. The wet, green taste. Memories of fear and loss and affection.

Moments like these propel us into what the New Testament writers call a state of *anamnesis*—a state of deep remembering or, better, a state of unforgetting.[3] It was such a moment of unforgetting that allowed Paul and his converts to recognize Christ's presence in the eucharist. For him, as later for the gospel writers themselves, the taste of bread and wine, broken and poured out in *anamnesis* of Jesus, was the taste of God himself. To taste Christ in the bread and wine of the eucharist—in Paul's words, to discern the body— is to take your place in the history of his passion, and to recognize your own part in the story of his betrayal. To taste the bread and wine is to know God, and to know God in this way is also to know ourselves, in all our frailty and sinfulness. We begin to understand Paul's anger toward the Corinthians and the way they were conducting themselves. Treating the sacred meal with such cavalier disdain, they were not simply violating social decorum. They were consuming Christ's body without tasting it. Suppressing the memory of his passion, they refuse to *unforget*.

> Whoever, therefore, eats the bread or drinks the cup of the Lord in an unworthy manner will be answerable for the body and blood of the Lord. (11:27)

In the sensory world of the Bible, taste is never to be treated lightly. Taste, like smell, can signal an immediate encounter with the divine. The first English translators of the Bible were especially aware of this connection, because their own language had not yet lost the ancient link between

words for "taste" and words for "knowledge."
Take the word "savor," a word that the King
James translators frequently use to translate the
complex of Hebrew and Greek words for both
taste and smell. "Savor" itself comes from the
Latin word *sapere,* "to know," whence the Latin
word for wisdom, *sapientia.* In Latin, *sapere* in its
transitive sense means to taste, or to be able to
taste, and sometimes even to smell; but used
without a direct object it means to be discerning,
to be sensible, to be wise, to think. An obsolete
meaning of the English word "savory" (which
now means tasty) is to be "spiritually edifying."

Thus taste and smell, which rank the lowest in
the Platonic hierarchy, are linked etymologically
to moments of intellectual and spiritual discernment—and not just in Latin. The biblical languages—Hebrew and Greek—do the same. "O
taste and see that the LORD is good" (Psalm 34:8).
For the psalmist, taste is a mode of experiencing
God. Like the Latin *sapere,* the Hebrew *tam,* "to
taste," does double duty as the word for both dis-
tinguishing flavors and discerning the spirit. The
two meanings are often inextricable. The same is
true for Greek. The Greek translators of Psalm 34

(in the version familiar to most first-century Jews and Christians) selected the word *geuomai*, which functions in the same way as the Hebrew *tam* and Latin *sapere*. A related Latin word is *sagax*, which means both to have a keen sense of smell and to be shrewd or clever, whence that wonderful old-fashioned English word "sagacious."

Taste—know—discern—see: there is an instructive parallel to this complex of meanings in contemporary Hausa, the most widely spoken language in West Africa.[4] Unlike in modern English, where the phrase "I see" can mean "I understand," the verb for seeing in Hausa (*gani*) is seldom used to denote any form of knowing. Instead, the verb used is *ji,* a remarkable word from the point of view of an English speaker. *Ji* denotes the four remaining senses—hearing, tasting, smelling, touching—and freights them with both cognitive and emotional force. To know a language in Hausa is to *ji* that language. If one understands a point being made, one says "*Na ji ka.*" The phrase is best translated as "I hear you" (also used occasionally in English to mean "I see"), but in Hausa the feeling tone of the word is informed by the other three senses as well. Where we would say "I see," the Hausa speaker says "I hear, I taste, I smell, I touch." Our Western sensory hierarchy, which privileges seeing above all else as the means of knowing, is here turned upside down.

There is another word in Hausa even more emphatic than *ji*. *Ci* can mean to eat, to win, and to have sexual intercourse. It is used to express the deepest kind of understanding. Charged with pleasurable and erotic connotations, the word *ci* denotes the act of knowing someone or something fully. Knowing in Hausa is thus an act of the whole body, all the senses working together. As one proverb puts it, *Jiki ya fi kunne ji:* The body is better at *ji* than the ears. To see (*gani*) is not to know, perhaps because seeing implies a distance between the knower and the known. Another proverb puts it memorably. *Gani ba ci ba.* Seeing is not eating.

Such a range of meanings persists in the everyday modern English use of "taste," but only in a watered-down state. When we talk about taste in anything but a physiological way, we are usually making a social comment—"He has bad taste"— not an intellectual or theological one. Our metaphorical notions of taste are loaded down with presuppositions about social class and the nature of good breeding. Although we might think of such judgments of taste as discerning, they do not usually exhibit the kind of spiritual discernment that the psalmist enjoyed, or that Paul expected of the Corinthians, or that, for different reasons, is an everyday concern in Niger. Especially in a time like ours, when standards of intellectual and moral judgment are so diverse and contradictory, the Bible's use of taste as a theological category is a puzzle. For most us, taste is a relative matter, and judgments of good taste tend to fall in the sole domain of cultural snobs or cynics.

An episode in John Milton's *Paradise Lost* shows how far we have strayed from the biblical meanings of taste as discernment or moral guide. Milton was a gifted reader of scripture, with an ear keenly attuned to the nuances of Hebrew and Greek. In *Paradise Lost,* Milton retells the Genesis story of Adam and Eve as a study in the failure of taste—taste not as an aesthetic matter, but as a matter of moral discernment. In the world the poem creates (and whose loss the poem laments), tasting is allied to moral sense, and the lapse of taste is mortal. Early in Book V of the poem, long before Satan appears to tempt her directly, Eve tells Adam of a strange dream she has had about the "interdicted tree of knowledge." An angel appeared to her (whom the wary reader knows already to be Satan in disguise) and, to her surprise, sang the praises of the forbidden tree. "Taste this," the angel said to her, "and be henceforth among the gods / Thyself a goddess." The false angel deliberately confused physical taste with spiritual discernment, in a way that prepared the unwitting Eve to succumb to the real temptation that will follow. The physical taste of the fruit will magically endow her with god-like knowledge, "savor" (*sapor*) with *sapientia*. The apple in her dream had "a pleasant, savory smell," which she "could not but taste."

Of course, had Eve spoken Latin (or Hausa!), she would have recognized this pun on "savory" and sapientia, and recognized what danger she was in. Milton's dream-angel reduces taste to a purely physical matter—a means of pleasure without consequences. As happens so often in Paradise Lost, the facts are clearer to us, fallen readers that we are, than to Eve and Adam in their innocence. In an earthly paradise where the knowledge of God and the pleasures of nature are interchangeable, there is no reason to distinguish between what you taste and what you know. Besides, Eve's vision of forbidden tasting had occurred to her only in a dream, and dreams (at least before Freud) were notoriously unreliable guides to behavior. In her still unfallen state, she is oblivious to the puns and double meanings that pepper the dream-angel's rhetoric. But after the fall, when she tastes the fruit in fact and not in dream, her own speech, and Adam's too, puns just as deceptively as the angel's. By the time the real temptation occurs in the poem, the ancient pun linking taste to divine discernment, sapor to sapientia, is distorted beyond recognition, producing disastrous consequences. The taste of the fruit acts like a verbal poison, mortally infecting their speech. In Book IX, Adam says as he chews:

> Eve, now I see that thou art exact of taste,
> And elegant, of sapience no small part,
> Since to each meaning savor we apply,
> And palate call judicious.

As we listen to this speech, which is full of puns and double entendres, words and their meanings begin to slip and slide. Take that word "elegant," which comes from the Latin word for choice. This episode is all about making moral choices, but using the word elegant in this way strips choice of its dignity—it becomes a matter of aesthetic rather than of moral judgment. Once he has eaten the forbidden fruit, Adam wantonly mistakes pleasurable feelings for moral sense. His almost devilish wordplay drains a word like "sapience" of its ancient gravity. What once was *sapientia* is now mere *sapor,* and the true meanings of words become just a matter of taste—"to each meaning savor we apply."

ॐ

There is a wonderful fresco of the Last Supper in Florence, on a wall of the monastic refectory in the old convent of Sant'Apollonia. The painter was Andrea del Castagno, and the fresco, thirty-two feet wide and at least ten feet high, covers the entire lower half of the wall, right to the edge of the wainscoting. Although Castagno painted the mural in the mid-fifteenth century, it was all but invisible for over four hundred years. Sant'Apollonia housed an order of cloistered nuns, and their refectory—along with Castagno's fresco—was off-limits to outsiders until the 1860s, when the secular armies of the Risorgimento opened such forbidden spaces for all the world to see.[5]

I wonder what went through the soldiers' minds when they first encountered this strange and marvelous picture. Jesus and eleven of his apostles are depicted seated on a stone bench behind a long table. A stiff white tablecloth extends almost the entire width of the painting. Its blankness makes you feel a bit uneasy, as if someone has vandalized the painting with a meticulously calibrated slash of whitewash. The legs of the table are all but invisible. The tablecloth seems to float in midair, bisecting the bodies of the apostles seated there. Unlike the figures in Leonardo's more famous version of the Last Supper, now sadly decaying in a Milanese convent, the apostles are not arranged around the table in significant groups of threes. Except for one little group, each participant seems caught up in his own space, every man isolated in his own private drama. The décor is spare and classical, the artist's palette (except for that brilliant strip of white tablecloth) muted, sepulchral. Six large, square marble panels, painted with extraordinary verisimilitude, line the wall just above and behind the apostles' heads. Two carved griffins crouch sphinx-like at either end of the bench, like tutelary spirits, heightening the moment's ominous stillness.

For all that, the painting is deeply theatrical. It is as if the artist imagined the Last Supper taking place on a proscenium stage. Castagno painted the three walls, the ceiling, and the floor in masterful, if slightly skewed, *trompe l'oeil* perspective. But the fourth wall—the one separating us from the action—is missing. You sense uneasily that you are not just a spectator, but a possible participant in the tableau being enacted—that the room being depicted is actually an alcove of the room where you stand. You have to wonder: Were the nuns' tables set parallel to the table in the picture? Did the nuns have the uneasy feeling, day in and day out, that they were themselves a part of this scene?

It is a sobering thought. Because one figure, and one figure only, sits on the viewers' side of the table, just to the left of center. That figure is Judas, perched precariously on a stool, sitting in profile directly across from Jesus. Judas gazes off to the right, already detached from the scene. His ears are beginning to elongate, as a mark of Satan's invisible entrance into him. Jesus' eyes are lowered. He contemplates the piece of bread soaked in wine that he has just offered to Judas, as well as the bread and wine he is about to bless and share as his own body and blood. It is an explosive moment. Peter, to Jesus' right, stares at the exchange in disbelief, while the beloved disciple, seemingly oblivious to everything, rests his head on his hands, and leans against Jesus' chest. As if to underscore the centrality of this grouping, Castagno has veined the marble panel directly behind in a violent, fractal pattern, a stormy chaos of red, white, orange, and yellow—in dramatic contrast to the sober hue and texture of the five panels behind the other apostles.

Castagno's source for this scene is John's gospel (13:26). He imagines the precise moment when Jesus offers the bread dipped in wine to Judas—a moment that the spectator, sitting at table, is invited to contemplate day in and day out. It is a painting—and a setting—that forces you to ponder the act of tasting as an act of knowledge.

When Jesus handed Judas the bread dipped in wine, what did Judas taste—or rather, what did Judas know? Except for Peter, perhaps, those in the painting who witness what is happening are completely in the dark. Would they have regarded the exchange—and Judas' imminent departure—as business as usual, just as they experienced Judas' objection to the anointing at Bethany? You realize as you stare at this scene that you know more about what is happening than the apostles do.

What does Judas taste? What does Judas know? The narrator tells us bluntly: Satan entered into him. I take that to mean that Judas made his choice, in a moment of stark exposure. To taste God is to know God, as fully as we are known. To know God is to taste God, in all God's glory and terror. Like Castagno's painting on the refectory wall, John's gospel moves us to ask what we would do if we were at that table, and Jesus had offered the wine-soaked bread to us. At the awful moment of crisis, when we find ourselves poised to betray others, stuck fast in our own resentment of those who have betrayed us, could we abide the taste of self-knowledge and self-exposure that Jesus offers—in the stark intimacies of his own self-giving? Could we allow Christ to transform our morsel of betrayal into life-giving bread, or would we cling to the morsel like Judas fleeing Christ's presence, with the taste of dust and ashes in our mouths? What place would we have taken in the history of Christ's passion?

As those Florentine nuns must have known, sharing meals day in and day out in the shadow of Castagno's formidable painting, this tasting God is a dangerous business. *Gani ba ci ba.* Seeing is not eating.

෩

Teach me, and I will be silent;
  make me understand how I have
    gone wrong.
How forceful are honest words!
  But your reproof, what does it reprove?
Do you think that you can reprove words,
  as if the speech of the desperate were
    wind?
You would even cast lots over the orphan,
  and bargain over your friend.
But now, be pleased to look at me;
  for I will not lie to your face.
Turn, I pray, let no wrong be done.
  Turn now, my vindication is at stake.
Is there any wrong on my tongue?
  Cannot my taste discern calamity?

(JOB 6:24-30)

How sweet are your words to my taste,
sweeter than honey to my mouth!
Through your precepts I get
understanding;
therefore I hate every false way.

(PSALM 119:103-104)

66

Your words were found, and I ate them,
and your words became to me a joy
and the delight of my heart.

(JEREMIAH 15:16)

three

The Touch of God

A FEW YEARS AGO, I organized a symposium on physician-assisted suicide. My job was to moderate a discussion between a psychiatrist in my parish and a distinguished Manhattan ethicist. Jewish but not particularly observant, the ethicist's background and experience led me to believe that she favored some statutory leeway for doctors and patients struggling to do what is right in the face of intractable pain.

I was mistaken. Her reservations ran deep. So many people she had encountered who desperately talked of ending treatment did so because they felt isolated in their pain. Some talked about themselves in the past tense, as if they were dead already. In the end-stages of their disease, they felt as untouchable as a corpse. But sometimes, she said, just a gentle touch of the hand could change their mood dramatically, breaking their isolation. Talk of suicide—physician-assisted or otherwise— would suddenly cease. Falling silent, she stared at me, almost accusingly. "Don't you Christians have a tradition of touching people," she quietly asked, "of touching with a healing touch?"

Her question sticks with me. I think of Mark's short and tumultuous gospel. It is early on in the story, and Jesus has emerged like a whirlwind from the wilderness—commandeering disciples, curing the possessed, attracting crowds of both the sick and the demon-haunted. The evangelist seems breathless recounting it all. Out of nowhere a leper appears, kneeling in the dust, demanding to be healed. "If you choose," he says to Jesus, "you can make me clean" (1:40).

Reading these words has the same effect on me as the ethicist's stare. "If you choose, you can make me clean." I had thought that freedom of choice was what the whole suicide controversy was about, choosing to die in your own way, at your own time, with as much palliative help as you can find, licensed or otherwise. But Mark's story is not about the leper's choice. It is about the healer's. It is a story about God *choosing* to touch. "Moved with pity, Jesus stretched out his hand and touched him, and said to him, 'I do choose. Be made clean!'" (Mark 1:41).

69

It is important to realize that the skin Jesus chose to touch was not afflicted with what today we call leprosy, or Hansen's disease. In Jesus' day, leprosy was a more general term. Any number of skin diseases would qualify. It seems illogical at first, perhaps, but the social and ritual costs of skin disease were as devastating as the physical— sometimes, depending on the disease, even more devastating. The priestly code in the book of Leviticus provides not only for the ritual cleansing of lepers, but also of leprous clothing and even houses (Leviticus 13-14). Holiness meant whole-ness, and a disease of the skin betokened a breach in the wall separating the clean from the unclean, the whole from the less-than-whole.

So when Jesus chooses to touch the leper he is not just curing him of chronic eczema or psoria-sis. Nor is he simply forgiving the man's sins, although most people would have assumed that the leper's crawling skin was both the result and the sign of sinfulness. By stretching out his hand and touching the leper, Jesus muddies the bound-ary separating the clean from the unclean, what is socially acceptable from what is socially anathema.

Such a touch has political as well as therapeu-tic implications. In effect, it redefines how God acts in the world. Jesus tells the man he is to show himself to the priests, thus starting a process of political and social reintegration that will restore the healed leper to full status in the ritual system that once had cast him out. But Jesus' touch, as Mark describes it, is more powerful than even Jesus himself had imagined. Instead of going qui-etly to the priests, the leper spreads the news through all the neighboring towns. It is not a story that can be kept quiet. In the gospel's larger picture, the leper's new wholeness is a sign that the entire system that had separated clean from unclean is in jeopardy, about to be blown wide open.

Why should a skin disease signify so much? And why should an act of touch have such tumultuous effect? Because more than any other human organ, skin defines boundaries. It demarcates the boundary between what we are and what we are not, just as the party walls in my city row house separate what is mine from what is someone else's. The skin's boundaries are at once impermeable and porous, inviolable and immensely vulnerable. The smooth, flexible, supple integument that protects us so closely is also paradoxically the organ most receptive to the touch of others—whether a mother's nurturing caress, a lover's kiss, or a torturer's whip. Skin is the organ of touch, and as such can be both a very tough and a very fragile thing.

We know that people who are blind or deaf make exquisite use of touch. Helen Keller wrote:

> Touch brings the blind many sweet certainties which our more fortunate fellows miss, because their sense of touch is uncultivated.

When they look at things, they put their hands in their pockets. No doubt that is one reason why their knowledge is so often so vague, inaccurate and useless.[1]

It is hard to imagine surviving even fully sighted and fully hearing if you have no sensation on your skin. Thomas Aquinas thought that touch was the foundation of the other senses. Contemporary anthropologists like Ashley Montague bear him out. Montague notes that there are fourteen full columns in the *Oxford English Dictionary* listing the array of words and phrases related to notions of touch. Such an abundance of connotations, he writes, testifies to the vast influence that the tactile experience of hands and fingers has had upon our imagery and our speech. A passage of music "touches" us; angered, we are "touched to the quick"; lonely, we try to "keep in touch."[2]

Jesus touches people. He rubs saliva into the eyes of a blind man, and lays hands on him twice, and the man sees. He puts his finger into the ears of a deaf man, spits and touches his tongue, and the man hears and speaks. He takes Simon Peter's mother-in-law by the hand and raises her from her sickbed. He takes the daughter of Jairus by the hand and revives her from the dead. Even as he is arrested, and rude hands are laid upon him, he touches the ear of the high priest's slave (which Peter in blind anger had severed with his sword) and restores it to what it was. "What deeds of power," people exclaim, "are being done by his hands!" (Mark 6:2).

But Jesus' touch in the gospels is not just about restoring the sick to bodily health. One of the most dramatic incidents of Jesus touching—his washing the feet of his disciples—has little to do with bodily healing. John reports it as he approaches the climax of his gospel, when Jesus and his friends gather for their final supper together. Where the other three gospels place the act of *tasting* at the imaginative center of this episode ("Take, eat, this is my body"), John describes an act of *touch*. Jesus gets up from the table and, without warning, strips off his outer robe. He ties a towel around his waist, pours water into a basin, and begins to wash his disciples' feet. The action shocks them, perhaps as much as when he touched the skin of the leper. Masters do not perform a slave's job. Peter speaks for everyone, perhaps including us. "Lord, are you going to wash my feet?...You will never wash my feet" (13:6, 8). We want God to get close to us, but not this close.

I know from experience that solemnly washing someone's feet as Jesus did carries a strong emotional charge. For many years now, I have presided at a ritual of foot-washing on Maundy Thursday, the day in Holy Week that commemorates Jesus' last evening with his friends before his death. As moving and beautiful as that ceremony can be, at its heart lies a radical breach of decorum. It is always a challenge to find twelve parishioners who will agree to participate. We seldom allow people to take such public care of us. To expose our feet to be handled and washed in a public manner—as we are seated conspicuously in front of the altar, watched by two hundred strangers—is to expose an odd vulnerability, a *need* to be cared for. And if we expose our own need too openly, how can we deny the needs of others even more vulnerable than we are?

Critics have said that two of the greatest negative achievements of Christianity have been making tactile pleasures a sin, and making sex, by its repression, an obsession. They may overstate

the case, but not by much. In most Christian congregations I know, touching in church—even in
these days of sexual frankness and an often obses-
sive focus on health and fitness—remains a potent
taboo. People still remember the shock of the
1970s, when liturgically-minded Protestant
churches like mine followed the lead of the
Roman Catholics in reviving the ancient "kiss of
peace." In liturgies that in so many ways reinforced the inviolable privacy of individual piety,
worship had become a mostly verbal affair.
Encouraging parishioners to turn to their com-
panions and offer a simple handshake seemed to
some a blasphemous intrusion. Our public worship habits tend to favor self-protection, not self-
exposure. In spite of what Paul might have done
to adult converts in his own congregations, for
the most part only Eastern Orthodox infants are
baptized naked anymore. And although people
allow themselves occasionally to be anointed, or
to submit to the laying on of hands, except in the
Pentecostal churches the moment is often an awkward one. The sexual scandals among clergy that
have been exposed over the past several years
have made religious people even warier of physi-

cal contact in church settings. Fears of lawsuits and large insurance claims in a litigious culture have reinforced the taboo.

So it is no surprise that the Maundy Thursday service can be so difficult for people. I think about the feet I have handled over the years. They are seldom shapely. Most people use their feet hard— they are callused, misshapen, sweaty, and smelly. I have noticed, too, that feet never seem so naked as when the rest of the body is fully clothed. They are sometimes warm to the touch; I never fail to be startled by that warmth. Washing feet in a liturgical setting is both public and intimate. People are both symbolically deeply vulnerable and yet, in the safety and beauty of the liturgy, trusting and dignified. No wonder that Peter, who had resisted his Master's touch, should in the end offer the equivalent of his whole body, like a client to a masseur. "Lord, not my feet only but also my hands and my head!" (13:9).

But the gospels are not just about Jesus touching. They are also about Jesus being touched, particularly during the tumultuous final episodes of his life. Touching Jesus is the ultimate transgression of boundaries. To touch Jesus is to touch

God, and to touch God is to expose ourselves to danger. When Jesus cures the leper in Mark's gospel, word spreads so rapidly in the region that Jesus can no longer go into a town openly. People begin to mob him. They struggle to touch him as he has touched them, like the woman with the twelve-year hemorrhage who struggles through the hostile crowd to snatch the hem of his garment. "Someone touched me," Jesus exclaims, "for I noticed that power had gone out from me" (Luke 8:46). The bleeding woman, whose condition made her ritually unclean and socially unacceptable, was not the only one with the idea. "All in the crowd were trying to touch him, for power came out from him and healed all of them" (Luke 6:19).

The ultimate story of Jesus touched, of course, is the story of his passion. The gospel writers are famously laconic when it comes to describing the circumstances of Jesus' execution: "There they crucified him" (John 19:18). John's economy of expression matches that of his fellow evangelists, and only underscores the violence of the soldiers who manhandle Jesus. But even John, who of all the evangelists is the most careful to emphasize

Jesus' divine aloofness, presents a strikingly vulnerable Jesus in these final episodes—at once the glad recipient of human touch and its willing victim. Mary of Bethany anoints his feet with ointment, wiping them dry with her hair. The beloved disciple rests his head on Jesus' chest as all recline together, Hellenistic-style, to share a last meal. And then, in John as in the other gospels, the officers bind him, Caiaphas's man strikes him, Pilate has him scourged, and Roman soldiers press a crown of thorns into his bleeding scalp and forehead.

These episodes have haunted the way Christians have imagined the experience of touching Jesus. The suffering, all-too-touchable Jesus is the focus of countless paintings and sculptures from the late Middle Ages through the Counter-Reformation and beyond. Some of these images are beautiful, even sensual in their delicacy (think of Jesus' smooth flesh as Renaissance painters like Giovanni Bellini or Piero della Francesca depicted it). Others are grotesque in their realism (think of Jesus' surreally distorted arms and legs nailed savagely to the cross in Matthias Grünewald's famous altarpiece.) But depictions of Jesus as the all-too-touchable savior are not just a product of high culture. An impassioned devotion to the wounds of Christ was a hallmark of late-medieval popular piety, and continued well into the Reformation. Many representations of the wounds of Christ—some moving, some macabre—have come down to us from their shrines in chapels and private homes.

A number of these objects were brought together in a show at London's National Gallery in the year 2000. Several of the images on display were not for the squeamish. There was a ring from fifteenth-century Coventry inscribed with the five wounds of Christ. It was to be worn constantly on the finger, the very instrument of human touch, as an aid to meditation. There was a wooden angel holding a shield carved with disembodied representations of the wounds of Christ, described in prayers and hymns of the time as the "doors" or "wells" of salvation. A terra-cotta sculpture from fifteenth-century Florence, almost life-size, depicts the risen Christ not just pointing to the wound in his side, but prying it open, as if inviting the viewer to touch and probe.

Perhaps the most alarming object in the National Gallery show was a crudely produced prayer sheet from a Catholic region of Germany in the late seventeenth century. The sheet is divided into three horizontal segments. At the top, there is an abstract rendition of the wound on Christ's shoulder that resulted from his carrying the cross; in the center, one of the nails of the crucifixion; and underneath, a vivid, gaping depiction of the wound in his side. With impressive composure, a curator of the exhibition notes:

> To the modern viewer, the similarity of the . . . images to male and female genitalia suggests disturbing pornographic comparisons. The highly sensual, at times almost obsessively erotic, concern with the Wounds of Christ indicates that the sensual mode was felt to be a legitimate and effective means of entering into a relationship with the Christ of the Passion narratives. Even the libido could be redirected from its base concerns towards a proper and virtuous devotion to holy things.[3]

80

This crossing of the erotic and the spiritual may seem foreign to our more rationalist, discursive sensibilities, but as the exhibition catalog points out, tactile piety of this sort is not necessarily absent from even the least pictorial of our traditions.

> Traces of this devotion may be detected in the words of "Rock of Ages," a hymn still popular today, which includes the lines: "Rock of Ages, cleft for me / Let me hide myself in thee."[4]

Once you have seen that Florentine statue of the risen Christ holding open the wound cleft into his side, inviting you to enter his very body, it would be hard to hear that old hymn in the same way ever again.

༺

Many years ago now, when I was struggling to come to terms with my Catholic upbringing, someone told me that one telling difference between Roman Catholics and other Christians was the way they represented the cross. The focus of Catholics was on the suffering Christ; that was why all crosses in Catholic churches were crucifixes—crosses with a body attached. Non-Catholics preferred resurrection crosses, gloriously bare, their polished brass glowing in the sunlight of Easter morning. This was supposed to say something about the difference between Catholic and Reformed theology. I suspect, though, that a class distinction was being made. Catholic worship was popular, working-class religion—full of smells and hugs and noise. Protestants were more rarified and refined. No messy crucifixes, no votive candles or incense or processions in the streets. Just that sparkling, expensive, empty Easter cross.

These are caricatures, I know, but they bear an element of truth. Although I have been an Anglican for over twenty years now, I have to confess that these empty crosses sometimes leave me cold. For all our talk of Easter triumph, I think avoiding a representation of Christ on the cross is how many Christians shy away from confronting the messy realities of death and dying, and by extension, from confronting the messy realities of Jesus' own humanity. A deep aversion to messiness is evident in those tasteful memorial services held by choice without the body present, where you get the impression that what is left of the deceased is more a concept than a corpse. This sanitized view of death has always bothered me, in the same way that I am bothered about keeping children away from funerals, and avoiding wakes. Whom are we protecting here, and from what?

Growing up in an extended Italian-American family, I attended my share of wakes as a child. I still remember the cold feel of my grandfather's hands when I ceremoniously reached in to touch his body (the expected farewell gesture in my family) at his wake almost forty years ago. Those hands were holding a crucifix. I remember the moment as at once scary, sad, interesting, and instructive. But there was nothing morbid or strange about it. Nor was there anything morbid about my playing with the crucifix that hung over my parents' bed. It was about fifteen inches high, with a little silver body attached to a polished cherrywood cross. When you took it down from the wall, you realized that it was actually a cruciform box, like an ancient reliquary. You slid off the cross with the little corpus attached, and inside you would find two small candles, which you could use if the priest ever came to the house because someone needed last rites. Reflecting on these memories makes me realize how tactile my associations with Jesus and his passion really are.

There is a scene from the film *Places in the Heart* that makes the point vividly for me. Set in the segregated American South, the movie tells the story of a black boy who shoots a kindly white sheriff, by accident. The story is about what happens to the boy, but what has stayed with me about the movie is an early scene, when the sheriff's men bring his body home to his wife. They enter roughly and noisily, carrying the sheriff's limp body into the dining room, where in a sudden violent gesture, someone sweeps the table clear. The men lay the corpse there, as if it were a mortuary slab, and then, embarrassed and mournful, leave the house to the sheriff's wife and her women friends. Carefully, quietly, the women strip the body, and the wife begins to wash it. The camera dwells gently on the scene, both on the face of the woman and the flesh of the corpse. As

84

the wife touches her husband's body, cleansing it, even caressing it, we witness eros slowly opening into grief and loss.

The scene helps me make sense of the moment described in all four gospels when women are seen taking spices to anoint the body of Jesus. The women intend to touch every inch of Jesus' body—bathing it, anointing it, making the putrid aromatic, preparing a proper burial. By now all the men around Jesus have disappeared, just as they had from the house of the sheriff. This last piece of unfinished business, this messy yet essential task, is always left to women. Anointing the corpse seems a way of asserting control where there is precious little control, a way of putting the last touches on things just before they fall apart.

A few years ago, our parish adopted the ancient practice of washing the altar as the last liturgical action of Maundy Thursday. After the foot-washing, the eucharist, and a simple meal shared in the dining hall by the whole congregation, the people return to the church as Psalm 22 is intoned. All sit silently, watching as the clergy and acolytes systematically strip every bit of decoration from the sanctuary and altar—palms, hangings, candles, cloth frontals. The stone altar begins to resemble an ancient sarcophagus. At the last moment, just before the psalm draws to its end, a bowl of water is splashed across the table, and the priest scrubs it down, using a roughly tied cluster of dried palms as a scrubbing pad. It looks as if we are washing a grave, making the best of what is left to us.

Someone once told me that he thought stripping the altar seemed almost an angry act, and so in a way it is. But not quite. The action is also strangely consoling, like the women washing the corpse in the movie. It should be noted, too, that the water poured out over the altar has been mixed with aromatic oil. By the time the washing is complete, the smell of balsam fills the sanctuary. I have found, when it is up to me to scrub the altar, that my hands smell for hours afterward, right into the middle of Good Friday. That smell is not the smell of death. Balsam is in the oil used for anointing at baptism. The smell in the church at the hour of death is in fact the smell of resurrection.

That lingering smell prompts a puzzling question: If it was possible to touch Christ's mortal body, what would it be like to touch his resurrected one?

On permanent display at London's National Gallery is a magnificent work by Titian, painted in Venice sometime around 1515.[5] It depicts the scene in John's gospel when Mary Magdalene encounters Jesus near the tomb, and mistakes him for the gardener. She has come to anoint his corpse, just like those women in *Places in the Heart,* but finds that the tomb is empty. She confronts the gardener, demanding to know where "they" have taken the body. Suddenly, the gardener reveals himself to her as the risen Jesus, calling her familiarly by name. She reaches out to him, and in words that have echoed through the centuries, he forbids her to touch him. Do not touch me, he says. *Noli me tangere*—the traditional title assigned to Titian's painting.

The artist captures the moment when Mary has just recognized Jesus (he is still carrying his gardener's hoe), and has fallen to her knees in front of him. As she leans toward him, Mary rests her left hand on the jar of ointment that she has placed on the ground, unopened. Her right hand extends toward Jesus, aimed at waist height, as if she is trying to touch his loincloth. Christ's risen body, lithe and muscular, arches away from her. Except for the loincloth, Christ is nude, and carries what looks like his burial shroud draped around his shoulders like a cloak. His right hand is caught in the awkward motion of covering his middle with the shroud, in what almost seems a gesture of sexual modesty. These unsettling hints of attraction and refusal in the picture got Titian into trouble when the painting first appeared. Some people suspected that he used a notorious courtesan as a model for the Magdalene.

As private as their encounter seems (in both John's telling and Titian's depiction), Jesus and Mary Magdalene are not the only occupants of the picture frame. They take up only the lower left-hand third of the canvas. Behind the kneeling Magdalene, and to her right, a thick green bush grows at the base of a precipitous hill, through which a dirt road climbs by switchback toward the gates of the fortified city in the upper right quadrant of the painting. A lone traveler walks down the road behind a lovely prancing dog. The traveler approaches a crossroads where a second path, narrower and much less worn, stretches upward again toward the left. Bypassing the city gate, it disappears at the crest of the hill. To the left, in the middle distance just visible behind Jesus' shoulder, there is a glimpse of sheep grazing in an open field beneath an immense, dawn-lit sky.

It is a haunting landscape, at once ordinary and mysterious, separated from the action before us by a leaning tree that slices diagonally through the canvas. By placing the tree in that stark middle position, Titian also manages to separate Christ and the Magdalene from each other—the untouchable divine from the all-too-touchable human—at the same time that he celebrates their restored connection. He has just called her by name, and she has responded in kind, but still it is a painting all about boundaries. Some boundaries are reinforced: the fortified gates, the dividing tree, the retreating Christ—"Do not hold on to me" (John 20:17). Other boundaries have been opened up: the road over the hill, the dawn sky, and (although we do not see it in the picture) the empty tomb—"Why do you look for the living among the dead?" (Luke 24:5). In Titian's painting, Jesus' warning to Mary is not so much a refusal of touch as its transformation—the resurrected body, beautiful and intact, demands a transfiguration of human desire. It is as if, after the resurrection, the act of touch, by which we recognize another human being as if calling them by name, must now give way to something new.

A hundred years after Titian painted this picture, another master struggled with the touch of the resurrected body, and produced a starkly different response. The artist was the controversial Roman painter Michelangelo Merisi da Caravaggio, and his subject was the encounter of the apostle Thomas with the open wound of the risen Christ, as described in John 20.[6] The two paintings could not provide more contrast in both technique and tone. Titian places his two figures in an open landscape, and we must stand at a distance in order to take in the scene; Caravaggio's painting brings us into the very center of things. Three apostles huddle together to examine Jesus' wounds. Everyone in this picture—the risen Christ, Thomas, the two other apostles—is too close to each other and to us for comfort. You can almost smell them.

The artist has rendered the apostles' faces with exquisite realism. They are peasants—balding, clumsy, and roughly clothed. The strong light shining in from an unseen source brilliantly illuminates the furrows of their foreheads, and highlights by contrast the dark, intense focus of their eyes. An old tear in the cloth has begun to separate Thomas's sleeve at the shoulder—the elongated hole visually echoes the wound in Christ's side. Jesus is clearly the youngest man of the four, but he seems tired, worn—like someone who has just emerged from too long a stay in a sickbed. Unlike Titian's Jesus, he wears a flowing white robe. This, too, could have been his burial shroud. The robe seems to cover his whole body, except that he has pulled aside the cloth with his right hand to expose a sunken chest. With his left hand, on which a nail wound is just visible, he gently grasps Thomas's wrist, and guides Thomas's hand into the open wound in his side.

Into, not toward. It is very disturbing. In the gospel's account of this scene, it is never clear whether Thomas actually takes up the Lord's invitation to put his hand into the wounds. On this possibility John is silent. Many artists have matched the evangelist's reticence. The famous bronze sculpture by Andrea del Verrocchio in the Orsanmichele in Florence, for example, freezes the action at the moment of the invitation— Thomas's pointing finger keeps its distance from Christ's wounded but triumphant body. Caravaggio's Thomas, in telling contrast, thrusts a probing finger directly into the opening, plunging almost as deep as the first knuckle, and Jesus himself steadies Thomas's hand with his own.

Although the painting was instantly famous when it appeared, and often imitated, a number of people to whom I have shown reproductions find it difficult to take. Caravaggio leaves you feeling like a voyeur. He has rendered the wound in Christ's side in aching clinical detail. There is no sign of blood, but Thomas's finger (like that of a surgeon or a pathologist) has lifted the skin so that it bunches up slightly above the cut. Probing finger and gaping wound occupy the emotional center of the painting. There is no escaping them. But it is not only the clinical realism of the painting that disturbs people. I think too that it is the picture's latent erotic power, much closer to the surface here than it was in the Titian. One thinks again of that crude German prayer sheet in the National Gallery exhibition.

In recent years, Caravaggio's sexual orientation has been a subject of much controversy, and surely his own erotic history came into play in the genesis of this picture. A striking painting by the contemporary English artist John Gregory, called *Still Doubting,* imitates Caravaggio's image, only the subjects are depicted as young men in leather jackets and street clothes. The painting demonstrates the continuing fascination of religious artists with Caravaggio's transgressive realism. But to say that Caravaggio's picture has homoerotic overtones is not to say that it is all about sex, any more than Titian's was. It is, however, about desire—the desire to be known by God as surely as we are known, the desire to touch God as tenderly as we are touched by one another.

Both artists set out to imagine the touch of the resurrected body. Their solutions are in counterbalance, just like the two stories in John. Perhaps the way Jesus draws near to Mary and Thomas reveals the difference between men's and women's experience of touch. When Mary recognizes Jesus near the empty tomb, she is freed from the task of anointing his corpse, freed from the sad necessity of touch. With Thomas, just the opposite is the case. Only by probing the wound of the resurrected Jesus can he see and know the tenderness of divine love, the reality of the risen body. In Titian's painting, Mary cannot touch the risen Jesus, which allows her to see him better. For Caravaggio, who like so many men lived in a world where such gentle male-to-male touch was taboo, divinity revealed itself not by sight, but in the tactile experience of body touching body.

⌁

I am poured out like water,
   and all my bones are out of joint;
my heart is like wax;
   it is melted within my breast;
my mouth is dried up like a potsherd,
   and my tongue sticks to my jaws.

(PSALM 22:14-15)

Let him kiss me with the kisses of
his mouth!

(SONG OF SOLOMON 1:2)

Immediately aware that power had gone
forth from him, Jesus turned about in the
crowd and said, "Who touched my
clothes?"

95

(MARK 5:30)

four

The Sound and Sight of God

LIKE MOST PEOPLE I know, I am very much a visual and aural person—a lover of music and painting and sculpture, and a voracious reader since childhood. To read scripture as I have tried to do in this book—through the "baser" senses of smell and taste and touch—is to read against the grain.

For me as for most sighted people, reading books, like seeing pictures, is a visual behavior, usually private and silent. I have always disliked being read to, even in childhood. Silent reading was a kind of refuge. In an affectionate but boisterous and unbookish household, I could feel that the world was in my control (a rare thing in any childhood). Nothing could distract me—neither sound nor smell nor touch—although the act of reading Dickens or Shakespeare freed me to imagine sound and touch and smell and taste in ways more vivid than I had yet experienced, except, oddly enough, at Catholic mass.

It was only in college, when I tried my hand at acting—where reading a script was just a first step toward performing it—that I began to realize that reading is not just a visual exercise. Words printed on a page of a script are dormant things. They demand to be awakened, not just by the spoken voice, but by the participation of every bodily sense, in imagination if not in deed. Like all ritual experiences (and theater is still at its heart a ritual), performing a script, or even hearing it performed, is a kinesthetic experience of gesture, movement, and muscular grace. Good actors make the same demands upon their bodies as athletes or dancers, with every muscle poised and accounted for, every sense attuned.

I learned a similar lesson—this time about hearing—when I decided at the age of thirty-five to take up playing the cello after a lifetime of piano playing. Visual thinker that I am, I had learned to play the piano as a child the way I later learned foreign languages, by sight rather than by sound. In an effort to master French or German or Italian, I always had to picture the conjugated verb in print before I could produce it orally. It was the same way with music. This visualist bias makes me a very good sight-reader (a telling phrase), but a hopeless memorizer. Take away the printed score and I am fully at sea, no matter how often I have practiced or how well I think I know the piece. (I have always envied the great jazz improvisers, whose keyboards seem to be extensions of their souls.) After many years of struggle I realized that by focusing so much on the score, I had ignored the look and feel of the keyboard, and so had unwittingly distanced myself from the sheer physicality of performance.

But then I took up the cello, and suddenly the task of memorizing seemed almost instinctive. This was not just because for the most part cello music is scored with a single melodic line (single, but not simple!). It was because I had to learn new music through *touch* first, and not through sight. Playing the piano is also a matter of touch, to be sure. But playing the cello, you have no pedal mechanism or Steinway action working to your advantage. It is just your two hands, an oddly shaped piece of wood, four taut strings, and a bow. To make them sing, you must learn to master an all but infinite range of correspondence between touch and sound. You feel this correspondence in your left hand as you position your fingers over the fingerboard, and you feel it in your right hand and arm as you scrape the bow against the vibrating strings.

The student cello I learned on could produce a beautiful tone, but it did not come easily. The distance between strings and fingerboard was unusually wide, which meant that I had to exert an inordinate amount of pressure on the string each time I wanted to change a pitch. It was even more difficult to use what cellists call the thumb position, which involves placing the left thumb horizontally across the strings while the four remaining fingers press out the notes. The closer the thumb to the bridge (the little wooden arch that supports the strings at the widest part of the instrument), the higher the pitch produced. But the strings are stretched tightly. So to play in the higher registers, where the cello really sings, I had to exert an enormous lateral pressure on the thumb in order to press the strings down to the wood— no easy matter for a beginner. Calluses develop rapidly, but not rapidly enough. After one unusually frustrating practice session I realized that my thumb was bleeding all over the fingerboard.

Bleeding seemed appropriate. The sound a cello makes is fleshy. Just a slight shift in the way you place your fingertip on the string (a bit more flesh against the string here, a bit less there) makes for crucial variations in pitch—variations often amplified by vibrato, the effect created by the controlled shaking of the wrist and hand as you sustain each note. And then there is the daunting range of pressure and motion the right arm must master as it moves the bow across the strings. Once you have mastered the physical

100

challenges, the sound you hear is as close to the sound of a human voice as any instrument is capable of.

All this seems dry and mechanical in the telling, but decent cello-playing is neither. It was as if my life had changed. Memorizing a passage of music became a matter of sound and sight and touch all at once, very much like learning to dance. As I learned a new phrase, I sometimes found myself involuntarily singing with the instrument, instinctively adapting my breathing to the rhythm of the passage and the sway of the bow. This awkward, demanding contraption of wood and glue, horsehair and strings had liberated my ear and redeemed my sight. Memorizing had become a physical joy.

But then, just as I had begun to master the cello's stern disciplines, I found that another contraption—my ear itself—had conspired to betray me. My hearing had begun to deteriorate. For years I had put up with an annoying case of swimmer's ear. I was used to irritation and unwelcome ringing, and to the occasional sensation of hearing ambient sound as if through a wad of cotton. But this was different. A hearing test revealed that

I had lost at least a third of the hearing in my right ear, and could lose a lot more. The cause was otosclerosis, a disintegration of the little anvil (the stapes) that the ear hammer hits to send vibrations to the eardrum and thus signals to the brain. The cure was surgical, a procedure known as a stapedectomy. Much was at stake: even with my hearing restored, there was a ten-percent chance, the surgeon said, that I would have to live with constant tinnitus (a horrible word for ringing in the ears) for the rest of my life.

As the surgeon described what he would do, I could not help studying his hands. They seemed huge to me, if only because the operation he was describing seemed so delicate. How could hands so large and awkward excise and replace such a tiny piece of cartilage in such a narrow, inaccessible space as my inner ear? As it turned out, they could—his hands were as deft as a cellist's, and my hearing was fully restored. But the cure took several months for me to appreciate. My recovery was more traumatic than the surgery. I woke up from the anesthesia to an overwhelming roaring in my ear, which was densely packed with cotton gauze. The ear would have to remain packed for

102

days. My entire sensory repertoire was now completely out of whack. I could see, but I could not concentrate to read. Half my tongue was numb, and my sense of smell had become unreliable. The throbbing tumult in my ear was tremendous, accompanied by that dreaded high-pitched ring. Never had the act of hearing seemed so tactile, so physical, and so oppressive. I felt utterly self-enclosed, imprisoned in a roaring cave, in a sensory world gone madly awry.

When Jesus cured the deaf and healed the blind, he did not seem to make much of a distinction between the two. And in his own way, he was just as hands-on as my surgeon was. Jesus did not heal the senses from a distance. What he did was messy and direct—he was all about touching and rubbing and spitting. Think about the two healing stories that come at the midpoint of Mark's gospel (7:31-37 and 8:22-26). In the first story, where Jesus cures a deaf man, he is in the Decapolis, alien territory east of the Sea of Galilee. This is usually a signal in Mark that something unprecedented is about to happen, a new boundary is about to be crossed. People bring to him a deaf man who is suffering from a speech impediment, and the crowd begs Jesus to touch him, an action that is apparently rare in Jewish stories of healing. Jesus takes the man aside, puts his fingers in his ears, spits, and touches his tongue. In the next healing episode that Mark reports, people bring him a blind man, and again ask Jesus to touch him. Again, the technique is frankly physical—he rubs his spittle into his eyes and lays his hands upon him. The two most refined senses in the sensory hierarchy—sight and sound—are restored by touch, one of the lowest and crudest.

In the first-century context, this is not particularly surprising: the use of spittle was common in ancient healing stories. What matters, though, is that Mark puts these two messy acts of healing near the very center of his gospel. They function as sensory preludes to the episodes that immediately follow in tumultuous order—Peter's recognition of Jesus as Messiah, Jesus' prediction of his death and resurrection, and the great vision of Jesus' transfiguration, when he appears to his friends as most godlike, rarefied, and untouchable. This particular sequence of events in Mark is no accident. In telling these two healing stories when he does, Mark has a theological purpose: it is only through experiencing Jesus' earthy humanity that his divinity can be perceived. Jesus' disciples, who see and hear him every day, are notoriously obtuse about this, even more after the transfiguration than before. It is paradoxically the deaf (even those in foreign parts) and the blind who more readily come to hear or see, and thus comprehend, the good news of God's redemption.

When I try to flesh out these stories, I think of the deaf man, unable to speak, as inhabiting the same roaring cave I did after my surgery. Except that where my recovery took weeks, the effects of Jesus' touch on the deaf man were immediate. The shock of articulate sound must have been overwhelming. For me it would be like waking up from anesthesia to find myself in the middle of an orchestra busily performing Mahler's *Resurrection* symphony. Touch releases tongue; silence gives way to voice—and now no one, not even Jesus himself, can keep the man from shouting the good news of salvation. My joy in learning to play the cello, or even having my hearing restored, provides only a fleeting hint of what such liberation must have felt like.

The healing of the blind man seems more problematic. At first it looks as if Jesus botches the job. Some people bring a blind man to Jesus and beg him to touch him, even though this would risk making Jesus ritually unclean. As with the deaf man, he takes him by the hand and leads him out of the village. But his first go at spreading saliva on the man's eyes meets with only partial success. "I can see people, but they look like trees, walking" (8:24). The world is a puzzle to all of us, I suppose, but how much more so to someone who has touched and smelled both trees and other people, but has never seen either of them. The moment is oddly reminiscent of the slow progress toward the light by the prisoners released from Plato's cave of ignorance, or the confused shock of recognition experienced by Oliver Sacks's neurological patients in the book *Awakenings,* aroused from stupor by Dopa drugs. Jesus lays hands on the man's eyes again. The man looks intently and his sight is restored. All becomes clear—a fragmented world immediately coheres. Does the sighted man suddenly reclaim, or experience for the first time, what the neurologist would call the faculty of proprioception, coordinating the stimuli arising from his own body—acceleration, position, orientation—with an exterior world now available through sight? Did the restoration of sight trigger a realignment of all his senses?[1]

As noted earlier, Mark's healing stories always carry a theological charge, and these two are no exception. Where the disciples closest to Jesus have so much trouble seeing the point, the blind man's physical sight restored is a sign of insight that the disciples tend to lack. But insight is not just a visual metaphor. These healing episodes in Mark celebrate sight and hearing not as rulers of the other senses, but their equal partners. To hear God or to see God in Jesus is to know God, but the knowledge evoked in these episodes is not an abstract knowledge that leaves the other senses behind. It is rather an embodied knowledge, knowledge that reincorporates sight and hearing into the full harmony of the bodily senses. I experienced this harmony in a small enough way when I learned to play the cello. But these are not stories about the consolations of art. The mode of knowing in these Bible stories—the mode of *being* they describe—is not so much aesthetic as ascetic, a condition not so much of harmony as of holiness.

What haunts me about the story of the blind man healed is that, at the outset at least, his new-found sight is only a partial thing, like my hearing immediately after surgery. There is a remarkable psychological realism in the way Mark describes this moment; its pathos is underscored by the spareness of Mark's narrative style. "I can see people, but they look like trees, walking." That is all Mark sees fit to tell us. But when the man opened his eyes for the first time, with the compassionate face of Jesus hovering close to his own, why could he not see? What blocked him from recognizing Jesus' face as a face, the way an infant recognizes the face of its mother? Why could he not understand that what he saw in the first instant of seeing was the face of the very Godhead, incarnate before him in this strange healer from Galilee? Did he not see the same face that Mary Magdalene saw, or Thomas, or even Judas? About these mysteries Mark tells us nothing, only that the blind man's first glimpse of creation—and of the creating God—thrust him into overwhelming confusion. "I can see people, but

they look like trees, walking." No human faces,
much less divine.

It was a long walk out of the village.
   So he asked
Jesus, whose hand in his was
   sweaty, what things looked
like (would he know sight when
   it came?) and Jesus
told him that wheel tracks creased
   the road, that the sky
stretched, washed out, that his
   sandals striped his feet in the sun.

And when Jesus had put saliva
   on his eyes and laid
his hands on them, he asked him,
   Can you see anything?
The question asked by his mother,
   asked by boys throwing
rocks, asked by the man's own tongue
   in the dark.

The man looked up and said,
I can see people, they look like trees
   walking.

> Their eyes and their mouths are olives,
>   green and ready
> to be picked, their fingers shake
>   like leaves.
> The trees are walking, their feet are
>   breathing dust.
> And then Jesus touched his eyes again.[2]

It all rings true. I think that it is here—in the gap between our first confused glimpses and a cleared second sight—where most of us dwell when we try to imagine the face of the living God. No one has ever seen God, scripture insists. Perhaps that is because sight is not so trustworthy a sense as we usually presume it to be. This may be why the great Christian mystics have seemed so unwilling (or perhaps even unable) to describe their experience of God in visual ways.[3] Mystics in fact are notorious for the imprecision of their visionary descriptions, for the way they resort to the other senses in trying to describe what St. Augustine calls the *visio dei*—the clear sight of God.[4]

There is a tricky paradox here. Visionary writing can be strikingly non-visual. Not since the blind man's day has anyone seen Jesus in the flesh.

110

None of us was an eyewitness to these events. Our halting images of God are like the blind man's images of the people around him: partial, confused, like trees walking. The irony is that we depend upon the reading of these gospel stories— for most of us, primarily a silent, visual activity— to inform our sensory imagination of God. And most of us regard imagination as an inward seeing—so the word "image" implies. But the act of reading scripture—a visual act in and of itself— does not necessarily bring God close enough to us. Scripture can be a means of vision, but vision is not necessarily the end of it. That is why the great liturgical traditions embed the reading of scripture in the multi-sensory experience of worship—in the Word read and heard, in the bread broken and the wine tasted, in the gentle touch of an anointing hand. That is why, too, for so many people, scripture never seems more alive than when chanted in plainsong, or sung in the glorious polyphony of a Bach motet. Even as ardent a Bible reader as Martin Luther insisted that scripture was meant to be heard rather than seen. It was the spoken word, the Word broken open and preached, that would enter people's hearts.

[W]hen ... words, not nicely chosen nor prescribed, flow forth in such a way that the spirit comes seething with them, and the words live and have hands and feet, yes that the whole body and life with all its members strives and strains for utterance—that is indeed a worship of God in spirit and truth, and such words are all fire, light, and life.[5]

"Christ did not command the apostles to write," he said with characteristic bluntness, "but only to preach; the Gospel should not be written but screamed."[6] It is no accident that one of the greatest legacies of the Lutheran reformation was its development of hymnody, and among its greatest artistic achievements were the cantatas of J. S. Bach. As Luther knew, and Bach after him, singers do not just read scripture—they breathe it forth. Bare reading of scripture is never enough; it is a bit like mistaking the menu for the meal, or the script for the performance.

Our senses, like our souls, are always restless. No wonder that the *visio dei* in the mystical tradition is marked by the relative failure of sight and speech, and is so often described by recourse to the other senses—to the sense of smell or taste

112

or touch.[7] So the great visionary Hildegard of Bingen could say that it was by our nose that God displays wisdom, lying "like a fragrant sense of order in all works of art."[8] Or that Christ's presence in the eucharist

> is the same as if some precious ointment were rolled into some bread and a sapphire placed in some wine. I might whirl that around into such a sweet taste that your mouth would not be able to distinguish that bread with the ointment or that wine with the sapphire.[9]

113

In the end, of course, our bodily senses fail us. The deaf and blind whom Jesus healed would lose their sight and hearing in the grave's dark silences. But even such a loss as death does not close us off from the touch of the divine. There is a famous episode in his *Confessions* where St. Augustine visits his mother Monica as she lies dying.[10] In an extraordinary conversation, he and his mother leave the sensory world—"the pleasure of the bodily senses"—behind them. Yet even here, at the climax of their visionary ascent, it is their sense of touch that provides them with the metaphor to describe their approach to Divine Wisdom: "While we talked and panted after it, we touched it in some small degree (*attingimus eam modice*) by a moment of total concentration of the heart." In the instant it takes for the heart to leap (*toto ictu cordis*), ordinary sight gives way to a visionary blankness, sound to an eloquent silence—both sight and sound yield their mortal sovereignty to the touch of the eternal wisdom that abides beyond all things. Augustine writes of this vision, and by extension, of his mother's death:

> If to anyone the tumult of the flesh has fallen silent, if the images of earth, water and air are quiescent, if the heavens themselves are shut out and the very soul itself is making no sound... if all dreams and visions in the imagination are excluded, if all language and every sign and everything transitory is silent... we would hear his word not through the tongue of the flesh, nor through the voice of an angel, nor through the sound of thunder, nor through the obscurity of a symbolic utterance.

There will come a day like this to all of us, when our bodily senses fail us forever. Who knows in what ways God will then make his presence felt? But here, now, in the suspended moment between our first whiff of divinity and that full *visio dei* yet to come, we can still rejoice to taste and see, to touch and hear the mystery of God.

ॐ

Let anyone with ears to hear listen!

(LUKE 8:8)

But how are they to call on one in whom they have not believed? And how are they to believe in one of whom they have never heard? And how are they to hear without someone to proclaim him? ... So faith comes from what is heard, and what is heard comes through the word of Christ.

(ROMANS 10:14, 17)

116

I know a person in Christ who fourteen years ago was caught up to the third heaven—whether in the body or out of the body I do not know; God knows. And I know that such a person—whether in the body or out of the body I do not know; God knows—was caught up into Paradise and heard things that are not to be told, that no mortal is permitted to repeat.

(2 CORINTHIANS 12:2-4)

And I heard a voice from heaven like the sound of many waters and like the sound of loud thunder; the voice I heard was like the sound of harpists playing on their harps, and they sing a new song before the throne and before the four living creatures and before the elders. No one could learn that song except the one hundred forty-four thousand who have been redeemed from the earth.

(REVELATION 14:2-3)

ॐ

*Those who say, "I love God," and hate
their brothers or sisters, are liars; for those
who do not love a brother or sister whom
they have seen, cannot love God whom
they have not seen.*

(1 JOHN 4:20)

*Have you believed because you have seen
me? Blessed are those who have not seen
and yet have come to believe.*

(JOHN 20:29)

*For now we see in a mirror, dimly, but then
we will see face to face. Now I know only
in part; then I will know fully, even as I
have been fully known.*

(1 CORINTHIANS 13:12)

Endnotes

INTRODUCTION: SENSING SCRIPTURE

1. Thomas Aquinas, *Summa Theologica*, 75.2. I use the Timothy McDermott translation (London: Eyre and Spottiswood, 1989), 108.

2. Hans Urs von Balthasar, *The Glory of the Lord: A Theological Aesthetics.* "I: Seeing the Form," trans. Erasmo Leiva-Merikakis (San Francisco: Ignatius Press, 1982), 369.

3. Jean Leclercq, *The Love of Learning and the Desire for God: A Study of Monastic Culture* (New York: Fordham, 1961), 19.

4. Ignatius of Loyola, *Spiritual Exercises*, First Day of Second Week (1541). Compare the fuller translation of Anthony Mottola (New York: Image Books/Doubleday, 1989), 72.

CHAPTER 1: THE SMELL OF GOD

1. For what follows, see David Howes, "Olfaction and Transition," in *The Varieties of Sensory Experience: A Sourcebook in the Anthropology of the Senses*, ed. David Howes (Toronto: University of Toronto Press, 1991), 129-147.

CHAPTER 2: THE TASTE OF GOD

1. For a pungent evocation of this experience, see William Carlos Williams's poem, "This Is Just To Say," in *Selected Poems* (New York: New Directions, 1969), 85.

2. Marcel Proust, *Remembrance of Things Past,* vol. 1, trans. C. K. Scott Moncrieff and Terence Kilmartin (New York: Vintage, 1982), 50-51.

3. For the discussion that follows, see Rowan Williams, *Resurrection: Interpreting the Easter Gospel* (Harrisburg, Penn.: Morehouse Publishing, 1994), especially 40ff.

4. For what follows, I am indebted to a splendid essay by Ian Ritchie, "Fusion of the Faculties: A Study of the Language of the Senses in Hausaland," in Howes, *Varieties of Sensory Experience,* 192-202.

5. I rely here on the description and discussion of Frederick Hartt, *History of Italian Renaissance Art: Painting, Sculpture, Architecture,* 4th ed., rev. David G. Wilkins (New York: Henry N. Abrams, 1994), 268-271. I want to thank my daughter, Liz Harlan-Ferlo,

for visiting Sant'Apollonia in Florence and making photographs of Castagno's frescoes for me.

CHAPTER 3: THE TOUCH OF GOD

1. Helen Keller, *The World I Live In* (New York: Century, 1909), 42.

2. Ashley Montague, *Touching: The Human Significance of Skin,* 3rd ed. (New York: Harper and Row, 1986), 128-129.

3. Gabriele Finaldi, ed., *The Image of Christ* (London: National Gallery, 2000), 166.

4. Susannah Avery-Quash, in Finaldi, *The Image of Christ,* 176.

5. The painting is reproduced and discussed in *The Image of Christ,* 172-173.

6. See the reproduction of the painting and a valuable discussion in Catherine Puglisi, *Caravaggio* (London: Phaidon Press, 2000), 216-219.

CHAPTER 4: THE SOUND AND SIGHT OF GOD

1. Compare Diane Ackerman, *A Natural History of the Senses* (New York: Vintage Books, 1990), 95. On proprioception as a "sixth" sense, see Oliver Sacks, *The Man Who Mistook His Wife for a Hat and Other Clinical Tales* (New York: Summit Books, 1985), 32-52.

2. Elizabeth Harlan-Ferlo, "Curing the Blind Man," a poem written about this healing miracle, from *What's in Between. 14 Poems,* an unpublished manuscript, 2001. Used by permission.

3. See William P. Alston, *Perceiving God: The Epistemology of Religious Experience* (Ithaca: Cornell University Press, 1991), 16, 20.

4. Bernard McGinn, *The Foundations of Mysticism: Origins to the Fifth Century* (New York: Crossroad, 1997), 232ff.

5. Quoted in Margaret R. Miles, *Image as Insight: Visual Understanding in Western Christianity and Secular Culture* (Boston: Beacon Press, 1985), 101.

6. Quoted in Miles, *Image as Insight,* 104.

7. See Constance Classen, *The Color of Angels: Cosmology, Gender and the Aesthetic Imagination* (New York: Routledge, 1998).

8. Hildegard of Bingen, *Divine Works,* quoted in Classen, *Color of Angels,* 59.

9. Hildegard of Bingen, *Scivias,* quoted in Classen, *Color of Angels,* 17.

10. Augustine of Hippo, *Confessions,* IX.x.23-25. I use the Henry Chadwick translation (Oxford: Oxford University Press, 1991). See McGinn, 234-235.

For Further Reading

Ackerman, Diane. *A Natural History of the Senses*. New York: Vintage Books, 1990.

Alston, William P. *Perceiving God: The Epistemology of Religious Experience*. Ithaca: Cornell University Press, 1991.

Brewer, John. *The Pleasures of the Imagination: English Culture in the Eighteenth Century*. London: HarperCollins, 1997.

Classen, Constance, David Howes, and Anthony Synnott. *Aroma: The Cultural History of Smell.* London and New York: Routledge, 1994.

Classen, Constance. *The Color of Angels: Cosmology, Gender and the Aesthetic Imagination.* New York: Routledge, 1998.

Corbin, Alain. *The Foul and the Fragrant: Odor and the French Social Imagination.* Cambridge: Harvard University Press, 1986.

Drury, John. *Painting the Word: Christian Pictures and Their Meanings.* New Haven and London: Yale University Press, 2000.

Elkins, James. *What Painting Is: How to Think about Oil Painting, Using the Language of Alchemy.* New York and London: Routledge, 1999.

Finaldi, Gabriele, et al. *The Image of Christ.* Catalogue of an exhibition at the National Gallery, London, 26 February–7 May 2000. London: National Gallery, 2000.

124

Friedlander, Wilhelm. *Caravaggio Studies.* Princeton: Princeton University Press, 1955.

Hartt, Frederick. *History of Italian Renaissance Art: Painting, Sculpture, Architecture.* 4th ed. Rev. by David G. Wilkins. New York: Henry N. Abrams, 1994.

Howes, David, ed. *The Varieties of Sensory Experience: A Sourcebook in the Anthropology of the Senses.* Toronto: University of Toronto Press, 1991.

Keller, Helen. *The World I Live In.* New York: Century, 1909.

Knox, Bernard M. W., "Silent Reading in Antiquity," *Greek, Roman and Byzantine Studies* 9 (1968): 421-435.

Kraft, Charles and A. H. M. Kirk. *Hausa.* London: St. Paul's House (Teach Yourself Books), 1973.

Leclercq, Jean. *The Love of Learning and the Desire for God: A Study of Monastic Culture.* New York: Fordham University Press, 1961.

Malcolm, Janet. *Diana and Nikon: Essays on Photography.* Expanded Edition. New York: Aperture, 1997.

Matthieson, F. O. *American Renaissance: Art and Experience in the Age of Emerson and Whitman.* New York: Oxford University Press, 1941.

McDannell, Colleen. *Material Christianity: Religious and Popular Culture in America.* New Haven: Yale University Press, 1995.

McGinn, Bernard. *The Foundations of Mysticism: Origins to the Fifth Century.* New York: Crossroad, 1997.

Miles, Margaret R. *Image as Insight: Visual Understanding in Western Christianity and Secular Culture.* Boston: Beacon Press, 1985.

Mintz, Sidney W. *Tasting Food, Tasting Freedom: Excursions into Eating, Culture and the Past.* Boston: Beacon Press, 1996.

Montague, Ashley. *Touching: The Human Significance of Skin.* 3rd ed. New York: Harper and Row, 1986.

Ong, Walter J., S.J. *The Presence of the Word: Some Prolegomena for Cultural and Religious History.* Minneapolis: University of Minnesota Press, 1981.

Orsi, Robert. *The Madonna of 115th Street: Faith and Community in Italian Harlem, 1880–1950.* New Haven: Yale University Press, 1985.

Puglisi, Catherine. *Caravaggio.* London: Phaidon Press, 2000.

Sacks, Oliver. *The Man Who Mistook His Wife for a Hat and Other Clinical Tales.* New York: Summit Books, 1985.

Sacks, Oliver. *Seeing Voices: A Journey into the World of the Deaf*. Berkeley: University of California Press, 1989.

Saenger, Paul. "Silent Reading: Its Impact on Late Medieval Script and Society," *Viator* 13 (1982): 367-414.

Visser, Margaret. *The Geometry of Love: Space, Time, Mystery and Meaning in an Ordinary Church*. New York: North Point Press, 2000.

von Balthasar, Hans Urs. *The Glory of the Lord: A Theological Aesthetics*. "I: Seeing the Form." Trans. Erasmo Leiva-Merikakis. San Francisco: Ignatius Press, 1982.

Vroon, Piet. *Smell: The Secret Seducer*. New York: Farrar, Straus and Giroux, 1997.

Cowley Publications is a ministry of the Society of St. John the Evangelist, a religious community for men in the Episcopal Church. Emerging from the Society's tradition of prayer, theological reflection, and diversity of mission, the press is centered in the rich heritage of the Anglican Communion.

Cowley Publications seeks to provide books, CDs, audio cassettes, and other resources for the ongoing theological exploration and spiritual development of the Episcopal Church and others in the body of Christ. To this end, it is dedicated to developing a new generation of theological writers, encouraging them to produce timely, creative, and stimulating publications of excellence, and making these publications available widely, reaching both clergy and lay persons.